Cambridge E

Elements in Global Dev
edited by
Peter Ho
Zhejiang University
Servaas Storm
Delft University of Technology

GOING PUBLIC

The Unmaking and Remaking of Universal Healthcare

Ramya Kumar
University of Jaffna

Anne-Emanuelle Birn
University of Toronto

CAMBRIDGE
UNIVERSITY PRESS

Shaftesbury Road, Cambridge CB2 8EA, United Kingdom

One Liberty Plaza, 20th Floor, New York, NY 10006, USA

477 Williamstown Road, Port Melbourne, VIC 3207, Australia

314–321, 3rd Floor, Plot 3, Splendor Forum, Jasola District Centre,
New Delhi – 110025, India

103 Penang Road, #05–06/07, Visioncrest Commercial, Singapore 238467

Cambridge University Press is part of Cambridge University Press & Assessment,
a department of the University of Cambridge.

We share the University's mission to contribute to society through the pursuit of
education, learning and research at the highest international levels of excellence.

www.cambridge.org
Information on this title: www.cambridge.org/9781009454094

DOI: 10.1017/9781009209588

First published 2023

A catalogue record for this publication is available from the British Library

ISBN 978-1-009-45409-4 Hardback
ISBN 978-1-009-20957-1 Paperback
ISSN 2634-0313 (online)
ISSN 2634-0305 (print)

Cambridge University Press & Assessment has no responsibility for the persistence
or accuracy of URLs for external or third-party internet websites referred to in this
publication and does not guarantee that any content on such websites is, or will
remain, accurate or appropriate.

Going Public

The Unmaking and Remaking of Universal Healthcare

Elements in Global Development Studies

DOI: 10.1017/9781009209588
First published online: December 2023

Ramya Kumar
University of Jaffna

Anne-Emanuelle Birn
University of Toronto

Author for correspondence: Ramya Kumar, ramyak@univ.jfn.ac.lk

Abstract: This Element highlights the pivotal role of corporate players in universal health coverage ideologies and implementation, and critically examines social innovation-driven approaches to expanding primary care in low-income settings. It first traces the evolving meanings of universal health/healthcare in global health politics and policy, analysing their close, often hidden, intertwining with corporate interests and exigencies. It then juxtaposes three social innovations targeting niche "markets" for lower-cost services in the Majority World, against three present-day examples of publicly financed and delivered primary healthcare (PHC), demonstrating what corporatization does to PHC, within deeply entrenched colonial-capitalist structures and discourses that normalize inferior care, private profit, and dispossession of peoples.

Keywords: universal health coverage, corporatisation of healthcare, low- and middle-income countries, primary healthcare, decolonising global health

ISBNs: 9781009454094 (HB), 9781009209571 (PB), 9781009209588 (OC)
ISSNs: 2634-0313 (online), 2634-0305 (print)

Contents

1 Setting the Stage

The private sector is well-positioned to contribute to the [universal health coverage-UHC] effort and already provides health products and services for many millions of people and communities globally . . . The for-profit private sector offers a diverse range of health and related products, services, and innovation. It provides over 60% of health services in some countries.
—UHC2030 Private Sector Constituency

This snippet from the introduction to the inaugural UHC2030 Private Sector Constituency Statement signals the role envisaged for the private sector – especially its for-profit arm – by UHC2030, a high-profile global 'multi-stakeholder platform' for advocacy and action on UHC (UHC2030 n.d.a). Aimed at accelerating progress on UHC, the platform convenes governments, multilateral organizations, philanthropies, civil society, and academics, atop private sector constituencies. The latter are represented by healthcare industry giants, such as Apollo Hospitals, Astra Zeneca, GlaxoSmithKline (GSK), Johnson & Johnson, Meditronic Labs, Merck, Novartis, Pfizer, Roche, and Royal Phillips, to name a few (UHC2030 n.d.b). Remarkably, less than fifty years ago, the private sector occupied no such privileged position in health agenda-setting. The famed Declaration of Alma-Ata, which envisioned 'Health for All' by the Year 2000, held governments responsible for 'the health of their people' (World Health Organization (WHO) 1978), and made no mention of the private sector.

The notion that governments bear responsibility for health(care) emerged in nineteenth-century Europe (and certain colonial settings) amid the rise of industrial capitalism. Where labour unions were organized, they demanded a host of government-purveyed health and social protections. Preceding and accompanying these demands, workers themselves, including immigrants to the Americas and elsewhere, organized mutual aid (friendly) societies to address collectively medical, burial, unemployment, and other needs. A more expansive organization of healthcare materialized after World War II, when governments in capitalist and socialist blocs, plus a number of decolonizing states, pushed by people's claims on the state, invested vast resources in health infrastructure and services (Birn et al. 2017).

In parallel, the creation of the United Nations (UN) system in 1945 and WHO (1948) provided a framework for multilateral approaches to addressing health (WHO 1958). Early on, WHO was heavily influenced by wealthier Western countries (especially from the late 1940s to the mid-1950s when Soviet bloc members withdrew). The major players – the United States (US) and Western Europe – shaped WHO's priorities around maternal and child health, nutrition, environmental sanitation, and targeted campaigns principally against malaria, tuberculosis, and yaws. Although some WHO staff members and expert committee participants favoured comprehensive, community-based health and social medicine approaches (Birn 2014a), WHO's primary contribution was technical guidance and related health cadre training (WHO 1958). As WHO's disease-oriented strategy became increasingly challenged in the 1960s, both by the growing membership of newly liberated states and the shortcomings of its hallmark global malaria eradication campaign, a chorus of member states – led by the Soviet Union – called for a more comprehensive approach to health services development (Birn and Krementsov 2018).

These aspirations were crystallized at the 1978 International Conference on Primary Health Care held in Alma-Ata, Kazakhstan (Union of Soviet Socialist Republics, USSR), at the time the largest-ever international health gathering. The declaration issued by the conference expressed at its core a vision for primary healthcare (PHC), which encompassed a broad set of values and actions addressing health equity, social justice, community participation, and intersectoral action, with their basis in the social, economic, and political factors shaping health (WHO 1978). Here, it is crucial to differentiate between PHC and primary care, which scales down PHC to 'a health service delivery approach characterized by first-contact care, ease of access, care for a broad range of health needs, continuity, and the involvement of family and community' (Kruk et al. 2010: 904) *sans* attention to social, economic, or political dimensions (Muldoon et al. 2006). Since Alma-Ata, the broader societal goals of PHC have been watered down by narrow and technical primary care approaches (WHO 2008a), which have, in turn, influenced and reinforced reductionist understandings of universal health, materializing in the current rendering of UHC.

As Target 8 of the UN's third Sustainable Development Goal (SDG) on health, UHC broadly refers to people having access to 'essential' healthcare services without suffering 'financial hardship' (WHO 2010a). Since its initial mention in a 2005 World Health Assembly (WHA) resolution, amplified by the 2010 World Health Report, and reaffirmation in various declarations and resolutions, including the 2015 Sustainable Development Agenda, UHC has become the number one priority in global health. Premised on the notion of *coverage* of a nationally defined 'package' of essential healthcare services, UHC presupposes a health insurance-based financing model and mixed public–private delivery. Focusing on healthcare service delivery (over health), UHC has dovetailed with and supported efforts to expand the role of the for-profit private sector in healthcare (Birn and Nervi 2019; Sanders et al. 2019).

Amply clear is that the private sector is now a key 'stakeholder' of UHC, heavily involved and invested in primary care (not PHC) initiatives spanning contracting, insurance-based financing, and consulting, all under the rubric of 'private sector engagement' (UHC2030 n.d.b). Notwithstanding UHC's patent subsuming by business imperatives, the rhetoric of universal health, including its lofty aspirations, is repeatedly invoked at the global level as a people's priority. In 2018, the Astana Declaration reaffirmed Alma-Ata's Health for All commitment, calling for 'Primary health care and health services that are high quality, safe, comprehensive, integrated, accessible, available and afford-able for everyone and everywhere, provided with compassion, respect, and dignity by health professionals who are well-trained, skilled, motivated and committed' (WHO and UNICEF 2018). A year on, the UN's 2019 Political Declaration of the High-level Meeting on Universal Health Coverage pledged to 'implement most effective, high impact, quality-assured, people-centred, gender- and disability-responsive, and evidence-based interventions to meet the health needs of all throughout the life course', including the vulnerable (UN 2019). Such buzzwords mask the 'on the ground' pro-business global health climate shaping UHC.

This Element was prompted by a desire to explore this contradiction in the rhetoric and practice of UHC: on one hand, the ambitious UN goal to 'Ensure healthy lives and promote wellbeing for all at all ages' (SDG 3), and, on the other, the entry and consolidation of a slew of corporate actors and agendas into global health, what we call corporatization or the rise of Global Health Inc. Broadly speaking, corporatization denotes a range of policies and strategies linked to the adoption of market principles, business logics, and managerial models, steered by shareholder interests, in the pursuit of productivity, effi-ciency, and profit (Farris and Marchetti 2017).

Alongside financialization, or the dominance of 'financial motives, financial markets, financial actors and financial institutions' (Epstein 2005: 3), corporat-ization has intensified the incursion and expansion of the for-profit private sector in global health (Stein and Sridhar 2018). Corporatization is broader in scope than marketization, which denotes the opening of healthcare to market forces (Farris and Marchetti 2017). It is also distinct from privatization or transfer of the responsibility for healthcare from the state to individual citizens, by introducing user charges, contracting out services, or selling state assets, among other measures (Armstrong et al. 2001). Corporatization is also to be distinguished from commercialization, which refers to the increasing primacy placed on commercial gain or profit in healthcare (Farris and Marchetti 2017).

The ascendency of Global Health Inc. can be traced back to the conjunctural shifts that took place in the global economy in the 1970s, when Western govern-ments embraced neoliberalism, an ideology and set of practices that gave prece-dence to business over labour within a free market regime (Harvey 2005). An early manifestation of its influence in international/global health[1] was the rise of global public–private partnerships (PPPs), welcomed by WHO in the 1990s to increase financing in the face of plunging dues from member states. Global PPPs – made up of intergovernmental agencies, private philanthropies and corporations – typically channel funding from donors to health initiatives (often disease-focused), all the while involving, and benefitting, private actors. The proliferation of global PPPs, and their prominence as a policymaking lever at WHO and other global health agencies, has been particularly championed by the Bill and Melinda Gates Foundation (BMGF, established in 2000), its own global health spending approximating WHO's budget in recent years (Birn and Richter 2018).

While historically, corporate involvement in global health concentrated chiefly on the manufacture, supply, and distribution of medicines and health products, it now extends to hospital conglomerates, private insurance, various contracting arrangements, and more recently, consulting firms enlisted in the business of helping governments 'fix' PHC systems. KPMG's Center for UHC, among the most active, seeks to equip governments with 'an unmatched suite of tools, intelligence, insights, and experience to make UHC reforms a success' by managing the rollout of insurance schemes, reforming governance, revamping remuneration systems, and striving to improve the quality and efficiency of service delivery (KPMG 2022). Such involvement enables the transmission of corporate logics and values – not least profit-seeking – to healthcare as was acutely visible during the Covid-19 pandemic, not only in relation to widespread vaccine inequity but also to the wretched state of PHC systems that were unable to respond effectively to people's needs.

Along these lines, the literature on corporatization, mostly from high- and middle-income countries, draws attention to the ways in which healthcare systems, even those that remain overwhelmingly publicly financed, have been reorganized to benefit investor/shareholder interests (i.e., profits). This work throws light on the ways in which business principles and approaches, including the entry of hospital conglomerates, the adoption of performance-based remuneration systems and cost-cutting measures, shape physician behaviour and patient care (Bagchi 2022; Farris and Marchetti 2017; Marathe et al. 2020; Salmon and Thompson 2020; Virk et al. 2020). Much of this literature focuses on hospital-based tertiary care in urban settings, leaving Global Health Inc.'s primary care ventures in remote and underserved regions of the world understudied.

---

[1] Drawing from globalization discourses, global health implies a shared global experience and responsibility for health, distinct from the hierarchical power relations connoted in the prior usage of international health (Birn et al. 2017). We use these terms interchangeably as we believe little has changed in the practice of global health.

Social innovation, an insidious form of corporatization, has served to draw vast areas of World Bank–defined 'low-income countries' (LICs) into the folds of the healthcare market. According to the Social Innovations in Health Initiative (SIHI) hosted by the Special Programme for Research and Training in Tropical Diseases (TDR), social innovations are unconventional or out-of-the-box approaches or solutions to complex global health problems, including the millions of people without access to healthcare (TDR 2021). Requiring fewer resources, and often involving task shifting (i.e., movement of tasks to less specialized primary care workers (WHO 2008b)), UHC-linked social innovations engage a diverse set of actors, including and especially the corporate sector, to deliver technologies to people living in poverty in underserved areas (TDR 2021).

To problematize the shift to corporatization and recentre the 'Public' in PHC debates, this volume explores: (1) How dominant understandings of universal health/healthcare have evolved post-Alma-Ata at the level of global (health) governance, and their interrelation with the shifting constellation of actors and forces shaping global health policy since the late 1970s; (2) the implications of social innovation-driven primary care initiatives for PHC in underserved areas of LICs; and (3) public sector-driven models of PHC that exist in World Bank-defined 'low- and middle-income countries' (LMICs), and perspectives and experiences to be gleaned from them.

We use a critical political economy of health approach that demands the centring of relations of power and the role of 'political and economic systems and key actors, and their accompanying values and priorities' in shaping health and health (in)equity (Birn et al. 2017: 289). From this perspective, health and healthcare, while influenced by determinants at the individual, household, and community levels, are also very much products of global, regional, and national forces, including social structures, asymmetrical power relations, political and economic systems, international agencies, domestic institutions, and social movements. Our examination ultimately rests on understanding who and what drives inequity and perpetuates inequality in health/healthcare within and across countries (Birn et al. 2017).

As we seek to counter dominant UHC ideologies and discourses, we are attentive to language. UHC, and global health more broadly, although purportedly concerning the entire world, remains focused on LMICs – a term that borrows from the World Bank's categorization of countries according to gross national income (GNI) per capita (World Bank n.d.a). This terminology conveys little meaningful information about each country, instead obscuring vastly different histories and political and economic conditions across settings. Thus, whenever not citing sources directly, we use the term 'Majority World', coined by

Bangladeshi photographer-activist Shahidul Alam, to avoid reifying oppressive and offensive categories and conditions in which the majority of the world's population is made to live (Birn et al. 2017; Khan et al. 2022). Generally speaking, 'Majority World' refers to places and spaces in which the colonial condition endures. Acknowledging the term's limitations, and the possibility that it underplays experiences of oppression of some made-marginalized peoples, we use Majority World to avoid reinforcing hierarchies and dominant ideologies, as imbued in the language of 'developing countries' and 'LMICs', while also capturing the spirit of solidarity linked with prior, albeit contested, terminology like the 'Third World' or the 'Global South'.

The title of this volume, *Going Public*, is a double entendre referring *both* to public financing and coverage *and* to the involvement of Global Health Inc., that is, companies that are publicly listed on stock markets and subject to fiduciary profit-maximization obligations. Here, the public also denotes the crucial role that people play in shaping and defining their healthcare systems, by collectively laying claims on the state through social movements and by exercising their right to vote. Thus, the title reflects at one and the same time our *critique* and our *vision*, as does the subtitle, *The Unmaking and Remaking of Universal Health*.

This introduction is followed by four sections. Section 2 charts the evolution of understandings of universal health/healthcare from the 1970s to the present, focusing on the emergence and refashioning of PHC throughout this period. We explore the interrelation of these understandings with the shifting constellation of actors and forces shaping the global health agenda. Using the Declaration of Alma-Ata (1978) and its progressive underpinnings as a launching pad, we examine the ideological realignment that began in the 1980s with the World Bank's turn towards user-fees and other cost-recovery mechanisms. We then review the 'Investing in Health' approach, introduced by the World Bank, which shaped the UN's Millennium Development Project under evolving privatization regimes executed by dominant actors at the global level. Lastly, the section explores the advent of UHC, a formulation that has enabled corporatization of PHC through calls for private sector engagement. By tracing the evolving meanings of universal health/healthcare in global health politics and policy, we demonstrate the close and often hidden intertwining of the global health agenda with private sector/corporate interests and exigencies.

In Section 3, we explore what healthcare looks like in underserved areas of the Majority World, focusing on social innovation approaches in primary care. We analyse three innovations, namely: (1) Chipatala Cha Pa Foni, a mobile hotline service in Malawi; (2) a Ugandan pilot project to engage private drug shops in managing childhood fever; and (3) One Family Health Rwanda, a franchise that places nurses in rural health posts. We examine the business models that guide these so-called innovations, and their engagement of for-profit private actors, to deliver low-cost health technologies. The section show-cases how social innovation does little to advance primary care, much less PHC, given patchy and fragmented (usually fee-levying) service delivery. As these innovations, by design, target niche markets in underserved areas for lower-cost (and lower-quality) services, we argue that they normalize starkly inferior PHC standards for people living in rural and remote areas of the Majority World.

Section 4 lays out an alternative conceptualization – and realization of – universal, equitable, and collective PHC via three case studies of publicly financed and delivered PHC systems. We discuss Sri Lanka's universal and public maternal and infant care system, Thailand's long-standing national effort to retain rural health workers, and Cuba's Family Doctor and Nurse Programme that has vastly contributed to the country's PHC achievements. Our analysis reveals that while each PHC system has evolved within its unique political and economic milieu, all are the result of decades of investment in public health infrastructure and state-led initiatives to train, recruit, and retain health workers. Despite current challenges, financing, administration, and delivery of health-care are retained, to a great extent, in the public sector in all three settings, enabling governments to keep costs down. We conclude that revisiting such PHC-oriented approaches is imperative to address healthcare inequities both within and across countries of the Majority World.

Section 5 returns to the Element's major themes and imagines another world of global health that values truly universal, public (in both financing and delivery), and equitable PHC. We argue that Global Health Inc.-led piecemeal interventions in the guise of UHC, while expanding markets, dispossess people of their entitle-ments to PHC. We call for a reclaiming of the public in our collective understand-ings of universal health/healthcare and submit that such a reorientation would require decorporatizing and decolonizing global health policies and practices.

2 Corporatizing Health for All, Step by Step

Notwithstanding WHO's progressive Constitution (1948) and the high expect-ations of citizens of newly 'independent' countries and other Third World[2] locales, these regions enjoyed limited advancement in public health in the decades following World War II. WHO, swayed by the development preroga-tives of the capitalist-bloc, focused mostly on technical disease-control

---

[2] In this section, we use 'Third World' to refer to countries that remained non-aligned in the Cold War context.

campaigns (penicillin for yaws, DDT for malaria, BCG for tuberculosis, small-pox vaccine, etc.), with health infrastructure needs unevenly addressed via bilateral aid of major powers in both blocs. Rebuilding after sometimes violent liberation struggles, amid many competing interests (e.g., education, civil bureaucracy, industrial expansion) and restrained by the yoke of unfair terms of trade and continued extractivism, left national coffers with inadequate reserves for public health beyond spending on urban civil servants and epidemics. A 1975 joint UNICEF-WHO study depicted the public health situation in 'developing countries' plainly:

> [T]he basic needs of vast numbers of the world's population remain unsatisfied. In many countries less than 15% of the rural population and other underprivileged groups have access to health services. More serious still, these people are both particularly exposed, and particularly prone to disease. A hostile environment, poverty, ignorance of the causes of disease and of protective measures, lack of health services or inability to seek and use them – all may combine to produce this sorry situation. –Djukanovic and Mach 1975: 7

The Health for All movement, underpinned by the Alma-Ata Declaration, was a well-intentioned effort to redress this situation. Proclaiming health a 'fundamental human right', and a 'world-wide social goal', the Alma-Ata Declaration decried 'existing gross inequality' in people's health as being 'politically, socially and economically unacceptable' (WHO 1978). Despite citing calls from decolonizing states to transform trade relations between 'developing' and 'developed countries', the declaration stopped short of naming colonialism and the capitalist world order as determinants of health, a legacy of silence that continues to this day, with far-reaching consequences for global health.

This section explores how dominant understandings of universal health have evolved since the 1970s and the interrelation of these understandings with the shifting constellation of actors and forces shaping global health agendas. In doing so, we analyse and periodize a selection of key global health policy documents and texts to shed light on the steady and ongoing privatization and corporatization of global health. We begin by outlining the political and economic conditions that led to the Alma-Ata conference, before moving on to the finer details of the Health for All agenda. We then draw attention to the incursion of neoliberal ideology in the guise of selective PHC, an approach that overshadowed social justice-oriented PHC initiatives in the 1980s. Next, we delve into the World Bank's 1993 World Development Report in which selective PHC was remodelled into a 'package' of essential health services, inaugurating the 'health as investment' approach integral to the UN's Millennium Development Project. Lastly, we discuss the advent of UHC, a formulation that has mobilized for-profit private sector engagement and corporatisation of global health. We argue that corporate interests underpin global health policymaking, normalizing starkly inferior standards of care for people living in poverty, while drawing in vast expanses of the Majority World into the tentacles of Global Health Inc.

Health for All and the New International Economic Order: The 1970s

The Declaration of Alma-Ata was adopted at the 1978 International Conference on Primary Health Care in Kazakhstan, then a Soviet republic. The Conference, co-sponsored by WHO and UNICEF, brought together 3,000 delegates representing 134 countries and 67 UN bodies and non-governmental organizations (NGOs). In gestation since the early 1970s, the declaration was shaped amid competing Cold War ideologies and calls for self-determination by decolonizing states, and signalled a radical departure from the disease-oriented technical approach hitherto pursued by WHO (Birn and Krementsov 2018).

Two decades earlier, stymied by unfair terms of trade and continued plundering of resources, Third World countries, many of them newly liberated, had begun to organize, both within and beyond the UN. In 1955, representatives of a group of Asian and African countries met in Bandung, Indonesia, to denounce neo-colonialism in foreign aid and demand respect for national sovereignty. This effort congealed in 1961 as the Non-Aligned Movement, formalized as the Group of 77 (G77, now including several countries in Latin America and the Caribbean) at the 1964 UN Conference on Trade and Development (UNCTAD). In 1974, pressured by the G77's demands, the UN endorsed the Declaration on the Establishment of a New International Economic Order (NIEO) (UN 2014).

Decrying 'the remaining vestiges of alien and colonial domination, foreign occupation, racial discrimination, *apartheid*, and neo-colonialism in all its forms' (italicized in original) the NIEO articulated, among other principles, the sovereign equality of States, self-determination, territorial integrity, non-interference, and the 'right of every country to adopt the economic and social system that it deems the most appropriate for its own development'. It also embraced the right to 'restitution and full compensation for the exploitation and depletion of, and damages to, the natural resources and all other resources' (UN 1974). Essentially, the NIEO was a broad demand for decolonization and, in particular, transformation of economic relations.

The extent to which the NIEO made headway at WHO was limited (Chorev 2012). From early on, the UN system and WHO were dominated by Western nations, especially the US and its allies (Litsios 2002). Dissatisfied with WHO's partiality in the Cold War context and the UN's failure to support the rebuilding of the devastated USSR, the Soviet Union withdrew its WHO (and UN) membership in 1949, only returning in 1956, but mostly pursued its foreign policy agenda outside the UN system. Even so, the 'Socialist bloc' was a formidable force and did sway WHO's agenda, if in a circumscribed fashion (Birn and Krementsov 2018).

The Soviet proposal for WHO's advocacy of national health systems was made when WHO's vertical malaria eradication campaign was under mounting criticism. In 1970, Dmitry Venediktov, the Soviet delegate to WHO, proposed a resolution outlining the principles for developing a national public health system. It met resistance on two fronts: first, the notion that states be responsible for 'providing' healthcare services within a 'national health service based on a single national plan', and, second, that healthcare services be delivered 'free of charge' (Litsios 2002: 712). Pressured by the US to drop the language of a single plan and free services, WHA 23.61 ultimately called for 'a *nation-wide system* of health services based on a *general national plan and local planning'*, and 'universally available preventive and curative medical care, *without financial or other impediments'* (WHO 1970, emphasis added).

Years later, the 1978 Alma-Ata Declaration contained no reference to national health services or free healthcare. The government's role was limited to '[formulating] national policies, strategies and plans of action to launch and sustain primary health care as part of a comprehensive national health system'. Nevertheless, the phrase 'comprehensive national health system' conveyed the notion of a single (unfragmented) health system, a far cry from today's mixed public–private model supported by WHO (2020a). Neither the Alma-Ata Declaration, the accompanying conference report, nor the joint report of the Director-General of WHO and Executive Director of UNICEF, mentioned the private sector, although the last cited the importance of coordination in settings where 'the health system is composed of multiple agencies' (WHO-UNICEF 1978: 73).

The Alma-Ata Declaration was sweeping in its definition of the scope of health. Portraying health as intertwined with economic and social development, the declaration defined PHC to include 'at least' health education, food and nutrition, safe water and basic sanitation, maternal and child healthcare (including family planning), immunization, prevention and control of infectious diseases, treatment of common diseases/injuries, and provision of essential medicines. More expansively, the declaration called for the coordinated involvement of a range of sectors in PHC, including 'agriculture, animal husbandry, food, industry, education, housing, public works, [and] communications'. Strikingly, it framed PHC in the language of social justice, and decried resources being spent on 'armaments and military conflicts', calling on governments to instead divert such resources towards PHC (WHO 1978).

The declaration favoured a bottom-up approach that emphasized community participation and self-reliance (Cueto et al. 2019), following on the then WHO Director-General Halfdan Mahler's experience with tuberculosis control in India. Mahler was wary of what he considered an overly medicalized approach to healthcare in the USSR (Birn and Krementsov 2018). Alluding to achievements of China's 'barefoot doctors' and the People's Health Commissions of post-revolution Cuba, the declaration called for the involvement of community workers and the broader public in PHC. Despite the progressive connotations of public participation, the emphasis on self-reliance foreshadowed neoliberal renditions of health that would place the responsibility for health/healthcare on individuals and households.

The declaration identified inequalities between 'developed and developing countries' (and within countries) as a threat to health, yet failed to name dire poverty, ongoing colonialism, and neo-colonial extractivism, all crucial health determinants in the 'developing world'. A call for the 'fullest use of local, national and other available resources' placed undue emphasis on domestic capacities, contesting the NIEO's call for international cooperation. Indeed, Chorev (2012) suggests that WHO made a strategic decision to focus on inequity *within* countries, instead of *between* them, to sidestep the issue of cooperation. Meanwhile, the declaration's support for universal 'essential' health care, 'at a cost that the community and country can afford', accepted different PHC standards based on contrasting economic conditions.

In sum, while the 1978 Alma-Ata Declaration departed from the narrow, top-down disease-oriented approach that was previously integral to international public health efforts, rival Cold War interests diluted its radical potential. For one, the state's role in healthcare delivery remained ambiguous, distancing the USSR's stance. Moreover, the declaration's reference to essential healthcare that countries could afford was seemingly at odds with (truly) universal and comprehensive PHC. Before these contradictions could be ironed out, however, Alma-Ata's ambitious agenda would be undercut.

Selective Primary Healthcare (SPHC) and Neoliberal Re-ordering: The 1980s

From its very inception, the Alma-Ata Declaration and its Health for All pledge were viewed as unfeasible by dominant international actors both within and outside WHO. Just seven months after the Alma-Ata conference, the Rockefeller

Foundation hosted a group of 'experts' at its Bellagio facility under the theme 'Health and Population in Developing Countries' (part of an ongoing series planned before the Alma-Ata conference). The meeting convened key development agencies, including the World Bank, Canada's International Development Research Centre (IDRC), the United States Agency for International Development (USAID), and the Ford Foundation (Cueto 2004; Segal 1980).

There, the Rockefeller Foundation's Health Sciences Division chief Kenneth Warren, together with contractor Julia Walsh, presented a paper titled 'Selective primary health care: An interim strategy for disease control in developing countries', soon published in the prestigious *New England Journal of Medicine* (Walsh and Warren 1979). Mapping an alternative approach to PHC, it pointed to the problem of 'diminishing resources', (p. 145), asserting that delivery of a selection of low-cost interventions would bring quicker reductions in morbidity and mortality until comprehensive PHC could be pursued. The latter, the authors argued, was impractical in the short term owing to the vast amounts of resources that would be required to develop health centres and train health workers in 'developing countries'.

Selective primary healthcare (SPHC) harked back to the vertical disease approach in its call for a package of low-cost health interventions that targeted specific diseases affecting poor women and children (Cueto 2004). Walsh and Warren (1979) recommended five interventions prioritized on cost-effectiveness, namely: measles and diphtheria, pertussis, and tetanus (DPT) immunization for children; tetanus toxoid for pregnant women; long-term breastfeeding; chloroquine for febrile children under three years in malaria-endemic areas; and oral rehydration packets with instructions (pp. 151–2).

Presented as an 'interim strategy', SPHC was swiftly embraced by a host of international health and development agencies, including WHO. Led by Executive Director James Grant, UNICEF launched its 'Child Survival Revolution' (1982), focusing on four interventions: growth monitoring, oral rehydration therapy, breastfeeding, and immunization, expanded later to include food supplementation, family planning, and female education. SPHC became entrenched through maternal and child health initiatives such as the 1984 Task Force on Child Survival, a collaboration of UNICEF, WHO, the United Nations Development Programme (UNDP), World Bank, and Rockefeller Foundation, and, subsequently, the 1987 Safe Motherhood Initiative, launched by the World Bank, WHO, and United Nations Population Fund (UNFPA; Rosenfield and Min 2009).

That the Alma-Ata vision was so readily challenged by SPHC reflects the US's ambivalence towards the declaration (Litsios 2002), as well as the shifting global political and economic landscape. Under a deepening economic recession, Margaret Thatcher came into office as the United Kingdom's (UK) prime minister in 1979, and Ronald Reagan as US president the following year. Both were stalwart conservatives whose administrations advanced neoliberal ideologies that espoused deregulation, privatization, cuts to social welfare, and a reorientation of the state in favour of private/corporate interests. As the US Federal Reserve raised interest rates in 1979 to counter inflation, Third World governments, heavily indebted after the 1973 Organisation of Petroleum Exporting Countries' embargo and oil shocks, were thrown into a debt crisis. Starting with Mexico in 1982, several Latin American countries defaulted on debt repayments, leading the International Monetary Fund (IMF) and World Bank to negotiate new loans – called structural adjustment loans (SALs) – to avert the spread of non-repayment and protect the private banking sector from the financial crisis (Harvey 2005; Prashad 2013).

Under the aegis of the Washington-based IMF, World Bank, and US Treasury – the 'Washington Consensus' – SALs specified conditions for economic restructuring: trade liberalization, financial re-regulation, privatization, weakening of public health, environmental, and other protective regulations, regressive taxation, and slashed welfare budgets (Harvey 2005). As governments borrowed more and more from volatile capital markets, Third World debt rose, necessitating further conditional borrowing and intensifying market integration. This exacerbated the dependent relationship between decolonizing states and the First World, even as it renewed the profitability of capital (Patnaik 1973). Various analysts argue that the debt crisis was engineered to rein in the Third World, and the NIEO, in particular (Prashad 2014).

WHO, meanwhile, became embroiled in controversy due to its advocacy of generic medicines (as opposed to patent-protected drugs) and its 1981 joint resolution with UNICEF on unethical marketing of breast milk substitutes. After the WHA froze WHO's budget in 1982 and the US slashed its dues, partly in response to industry pressure, WHO had to increasingly rely on earmarked funds from the World Bank, bilateral agencies, and non-state actors, substantially compromising its independence in later years. In parallel, the World Bank, which had commenced financing family planning initiatives in the 1970s, was steadily consolidating its role as lead player in the health and development arena (Cueto et al. 2019), spearheading healthcare reforms by mediating SALs and extending health sector loans in indebted countries (Birn et al. 2016).

Guided by neoliberal ideology, the World Bank's international health and development initiatives presupposed that public spending had to be curtailed. Its landmark report titled, 'Financing Health Services in Developing Countries', (FHSDC; World Bank 1987), identified insufficient spending on cost-effective activities, internal inefficiency of public programmes, and inequity in the distribution of health benefits (pp. 2–3), as critical issues affecting health systems. Citing inequity as a problem, the report undermined the notion of universality, perversely arguing that providing a single level of healthcare was tantamount to subsidizing the 'rich' to the detriment of the 'poor' (pp. 3–4), a wrongheaded theory that persists to this day.

In the FHSDC report, the World Bank proposed: instituting user charges at government health facilities, accessing non-governmental (read private) resources for the development of healthcare systems, and decentralization, among other measures. Here, it was expected that user-fees would raise revenue for health systems and lead the public to place greater value on services with a price tag; in calling for levying charges for curative services, the authors assumed that people would be more willing to pay for perceived benefits associated with curative (as opposed to preventive) care. Further, by compelling the wealthy to pay, the report argued, governments could 'free [up] resources' for the poor, for whom government-subsidized (private) insurance schemes could cover user charges (World Bank 1987).

The FHSDC report noted that the existence of free health services would not only widen inequity but would also impede expansion of insurance coverage; universal schemes financed by general taxation were discouraged to avoid subsidizing the rich (World Bank 1987). The report did acknowledge that introducing insurance schemes could increase health system costs but suggested that co-payments, deductibles, and other cost-sharing mechanisms, combined with greater competition among insurance providers, would help to curb wasteful health expenditures, apparently overlooking the disastrous consequences of all these measures in the US (Birn and Hellander 2016).

Decentralization, defined in the FHSDC report as giving 'greater financial and management autonomy to local units of the system', (p. 44) was expected to improve efficiency by bringing decision-making and budgeting close to the local level. Granting healthcare facilities more control over fee collection and resource allocation, the authors claimed, would translate to efficiency gains, primarily through incentives for local managers to generate revenue at their respective healthcare facilities. In practice, however, decentralization policies have entailed cuts to health spending and weakened the accountability of healthcare systems (Birn et al. 2000).

The FHSDC report's proposals were emblematic of the era's approaches and assumptions around healthcare. Sadly, even as WHO was still trying to advance Alma-Ata principles, the World Bank's health reform tenets guided the Bamako Initiative, launched in 1987 at a WHO-UNICEF-sponsored meeting of health ministers of African countries. Aimed at improving women's and children's health amid economic crisis, the Bamako Initiative emphasized cost recovery, especially community pre-payment and user-fees for medicines, as well as decentralization and community participation (McPake et al. 1993). Although some WHO sources described the Bamako Initiative in positive terms (Pangu 1997; Regional Committee for Africa, 49 1999), an evaluation five years on highlighted affordability barriers hampering service utilization (McPake et al. 1993). Despite putative advances in PHC 'coverage', user-fees, which had never been piloted, became a major impediment to accessing healthcare (Rowden 2013; Uzochukwu et al. 2004).

The Bamako Initiative and related policies were notably marked by the impact of SALs. In Africa (as well as Asia, Latin America, and the Caribbean), governments implemented drastic cuts to public health spending alongside directives to contract and outsource various aspects of healthcare financing, administration, and delivery, to the private sector (Baru 2003; Birn et al. 2016; Mackintosh and Koivasalo 2005). The ideological character of these reforms contrasted with the findings of the Rockefeller Foundation's *Good Health for Low Cost* study, published just two years earlier, that suggested a welfare and equity orientation, supported by state investment in education, public health, and nutrition, had been fundamental to the health achievements of the cases studies therein (Halstead et al. 1985).

In sum, the 1980s saw the rollout of SPHC in the form of low-cost primary care, mainly targeting women and children in 'developing countries'. Economic recession, SALs, and the World Bank's influential role guided health sector development in the Majority World, emphasizing user-fees and insurance schemes over public universal provisioning, with adverse effects on service access and utilization where it was needed most. Rather than learning from these lessons, the 1990s saw an amplification of this approach, albeit with several critical differences.

A Package of Essential Services to Advance Global Health: The 1990s

SALs came under heavy criticism from various quarters, including UNCTAD (1989) and, especially, the G77 (1989). The legitimacy of free market ideology was also threatened by the experience of the Asian Tigers – a set of countries that achieved high levels of economic growth 'despite' state intervention in the economy. The US Clinton administration, unhampered by Cold War tensions after the fall of the Berlin Wall and the Soviet Union's dissolution, carried forward a variation of the neoliberal agenda that now called for state intervention to address 'market failures'. The new approach, also informed by neoclassical thinking, pursued growth and efficiency, primarily by seeking to fix public institutions through 'good governance' mechanisms (Fine and Saad-Filho 2014).

Applied to the health sector, these ideas were brought to bear in the World Bank's 1993 World Development Report (WDR), *Investing in Health*, which depicted health and education as investment opportunities. Government involvement in the health sector was justified due to the 'positive externalities' associated with public health, mainly poverty reduction, and also market failures considered inherent to the health sector. Departing from the FHSDC approach, the 1993 WDR advocated *public* financing of both basic preventive health programmes and a nationally defined package of 'essential' clinical services. The service package was to be selected based on analyses of cost-effectiveness, estimated by disability-adjusted life years (DALYs) – a metric of the savings to be accrued from preventing disability and death from specific diseases. Extensively critiqued (Anand and Hanson 1997), DALYs have nonetheless endured.

Costing anywhere between USD 25 and 150 to gain one DALY, the cost-effective *preventive* health activities recommended in the 1993 WDR included: immunization, micronutrient supplementation, school health services, family planning and nutrition information, tobacco and alcohol control, and AIDS prevention. The attendant set of cost-effective *clinical* services, costing less than USD 50 to gain a DALY, included pregnancy and delivery care, family planning, control of tuberculosis and sexually transmitted infections, care for common serious illnesses in young children, and treatment for minor infections/ trauma, all of which, according to the report, could be delivered by non-physicians (World Bank 1993).

Coverage for non-communicable diseases (NCD), among the most prevalent in LMICs, would, however, be subject to resource availability. Specifically, 'heart surgery; treatment (other than pain relief) of highly fatal cancers of the lung, liver, and stomach; expensive drug therapies for HIV infection; and intensive care for severely premature babies' were not recommended for LICs (p. 10), at a time when HIV/AIDS was raging in Sub-Saharan Africa. The report called for cuts to public spending on tertiary care facilities and specialist training, deemed to 'provide little health gain for the money spent' (p. 6). Even as the report noted that governments of high-income countries (HICs) usually provided universal coverage of healthcare (p. 11), it expounded that the scope of the publicly financed package would depend on the income level of the country, once again explicitly normalizing vastly different healthcare standards for LMICs. As with SPHC and FHSDC reforms, the service package focused primarily on women's and children's health; all services outside the 'basket' had to be privately financed, regardless of their affordability (Laurell and Arellano 1996).

The 1993 WDR contained a noticeable shift in language, from the use of 'non-government' in the FHSDC report to explicitly invoking the private sector, and calling for its integration (including for-profit providers) into healthcare systems. The Bank urged policymakers to incentivise private healthcare utilization to 'free [up] resources' for the poor – by now a taken-for-granted strategy supported by little evidence, as demonstrated by the Bamako Initiative. The report argued that the private sector could be called upon to deliver elements of the essential services package on a fee-levying basis or with insurance coverage. Like the FHSDC report, it presumed that user-fees would not present an undue burden because they would be offset by savings on indirect costs, such as transport. The report also contained a series of other recommendations to bolster privatization, including the removal of regulatory barriers on competition among private providers, outsourcing water, sanitation, garbage disposal, and eliminating subsidies on these services, all in the name of equity. Among its key messages was a call to 'promote diversity and competition in provision of health services and insurance' through policies that support suppliers of public and private health services and insurance to compete in an environment where '[d]omestic suppliers [would] not be protected from international competition' (p. 6). Here was a blatant welcome to transnational corporations (TNCs) to enter domestic healthcare markets, later to be financed by governments through social health insurance (Hunter and Murray 2019; Waitzkin 2003).

Although a 1993 WHA resolution (46.17) urged 'developing countries' to 'mobilize and encourage the support of all partners in health development, including nongovernmental organizations and institutions in the private sector' (WHO 1993), WHO's official position on private sector involvement in the health sector remained unclear. In the first World Health Report (WHR), published in 1995, WHO drew attention to '[t]he breakup of the USSR, with the emergence of many newly independent states, the end of the cold war and the demise of communism [having] led to more emphasis being placed on privatization, decentralization, and liberalization', with consequent equity concerns (WHO 1995: 91). Yet, four years later, WHO showed support for partnering with the private sector under Director-General Gro Harlem Brundtland, who called for involvement of civil society and the private sector in the fight against poverty, and highlighted the potential of PPPs in combatting malaria (WHO 1999). The 1999 WHR proposed the idea of a 'new universalism' meaning 'coverage for all, not coverage of everything' (p. 43), and made a case for private sector integration to facilitate better regulation of private providers, presumed to be 'the first points of contact with the health system in many low-income countries' (WHO 1999: 43).

In sum, the World Bank, a prominent global health actor by the 1990s, framed health as an investment opportunity, shifting from its advocacy for cost recovery to calling on governments to finance a limited package of cost-effective essential services, while excluding crucial, but more expensive, services for chronic illnesses, such as cancer treatment or heart surgery. It ushered in the private health sector, presenting it as capable of advancing healthcare efficiency, quality, and equity in LMICs, and welcomed private domestic and foreign investment in the health sector. The WHO followed suit later, with PPPs serving as an opening wedge to involve private actors. By 2000, understandings of health and healthcare would be even further removed from health justice goals, framed primarily in the language of economics and business.

Business Alliances for Economic Development in the New Millennium

Circa 2000, a new and powerful actor, the BMGF, entered the global health arena, and, among other activities, helped ramp up existing global health PPPs and funded several new ones. The two biggest PPPs, GAVI the Vaccine Alliance, and the Global Fund, involving several UN agencies and diverse corporate actors, especially Big Pharma and their regional/country level representatives, were launched with BMGF largesse (Birn 2014b).

The then UN Secretary-General Kofi Annan launched the UN Global Compact in 2000, purportedly to foster corporate social responsibility (CSR) via corporate pledges to adhere to ten principles encompassing human rights, labour, environment, and anti-corruption. In reality, the Global Compact provided corporations with legitimacy and access to global health and other decision-making arenas through their affiliation with the UN. Alas, the UN failed to establish an effective system to monitor Global Compact implementation and corporate adherence to its principles (UN Joint Inspection Unit 2010).

Under growing corporate influence, bilateral and global health agencies concurred that governments simply could not afford to finance public universal healthcare systems. In the 2000 WHR, WHO unequivocally stated that governments were limited in their ability to finance health services, and referenced again the notion of 'new universalism' to underscore that universal coverage did not, in fact, imply that all services need to be covered (WHO 2000: xiv). The report cited the 'serious shortsightedness' of health ministries that focused on the public sector without regard for the 'frequently much larger' private sector (p. xv), and concretized WHO's newfound support for health insurance-based financing models by elaborating on the finer details of pre-payment, pooling, separating purchasing and provision, and so on.

The presence of leading corporate and philanthrocapitalist actors like BMGF at the table brought renewed attention to health technologies, while the social and political dimensions of health were eclipsed by an instrumentalist discourse that framed health as a precursor to economic development, now linked to poverty eradication in the UN Millennium Project (Fukuda-Parr and Hulme 2011). In 2001, WHO's Commission on Macroeconomics and Health (CMH), chaired by prominent Ivy League economist Jeffrey Sachs,[3] proclaimed that 'extending the coverage of crucial health services, including a relatively small number of specific interventions, to the world's poor' could save lives, reduce poverty, and drive economic development (WHO CMH 2001).

Atop the problematic assumptions of the health *for* economic development approach, especially the obscuring of poverty as a determinant of health (Waitzkin 2003), and the sidestepping of health as a human right, the proposed solution was again a basket of cost-effective interventions to be delivered through a 'close-to-client' healthcare system (WHO CMH 2001). As in the 1993 WDR, the service package primarily targeted women and children, with sparse attention to NCD control, such as low-cost health programmes to promote lifestyle changes and treat mental illness, diabetes, and heart attacks. The Commission also troublingly reverted to neo-Malthusian population discourses, presenting family planning, detached from social circumstances, as central to economic development (WHO CMH 2001).

CMH did not stray significantly from the World Bank's 1993 framework, even sharing its double entendre 'Investing in Health' title. The close-to-client system proposed by CMH was to be made up of a mix of state and non-state healthcare facilities, staffed chiefly by non-physician health worker cadres, who would deliver the state-financed package of low-cost interventions, once again reinforcing the view that different standards of healthcare among countries and settings was acceptable. Apart from financing the service package, the state's role encompassed: identifying the set of interventions through a consultative process, delivering the package at existing state-run centres, contracting private providers, and regulating healthcare services to ensure quality of care. Clean water, sewage systems, garbage disposal, food, nutrition, and agriculture, while necessary, were not considered in budget estimations (WHO CMH 2001).

How did CMH propose that governments finance this package of services? According to the Commission, cost-effective interventions had not reached those in need owing to 'corruption, mismanagement, and a weak public sector' (p. 4). Avoiding mention of how this weakening had taken place under structural adjustment in Latin America, Sub-Saharan Africa, South East Asia, and in the former Soviet bloc (the latter under the tutelage of Sachs himself), CMH called

---

[3] Jeffrey Sachs is better remembered for his role as economics advisor to countries of the former Socialist bloc and his advocacy for shock therapy – privatization, deregulation, and cuts to public spending – for these countries in their transition from centrally planned to market economies.

on governments of LMICs to commit resources and enhance transparency and systems of accountability, and for HICs to step up financial assistance.

CMH framed official donor assistance in charitable terms, further entrenching power asymmetries between minority and Majority Worlds. Although LICs were to receive grants, non-concessional loans were recommended for middle-income countries (MICs), to be borrowed from development banks. The Commission welcomed involvement of corporate actors, including Big Pharma, through new mechanisms for channelling donor financing, such as the Global Fund, dovetailing with the 2000 WHR's support for PPPs. Months before the CMH report was presented to the WHO Director-General, the heads of states of the African Union adopted the Abuja Declaration, pledging 15 per cent of their annual budgets to health, and urging donors to keep to their commitment of 0.7 per cent of GNI in official development assistance. A decade later, only two countries in the African Union and five Organisation for Economic Co-operation and Development (OECD) countries had followed through (WHO 2011).

In short, the turn of the millennium saw heightened involvement of corporate actors in global health and the UN system more broadly. Shaped by the goal to end poverty in the UN's Millennium Declaration, health was conceived of as a means to economic development. The 1993 WDR's proposal for a state-financed essential services package covered by health insurance and delivered by a mix of public and private providers, was revitalized in the 2001 CMH Report, and with WHO on board, set the stage for UHC.

Enter Universal Health Coverage

Although the notion had been in the making for some time, WHO's first concerted appeal to member states advocating UHC was a 2005 WHA resolution (58.33) titled *Sustainable health financing, universal coverage, and social health insurance*. From the get-go, UHC was premised on private sector involvement, reflected in the resolution's call for governments to capitalize on opportunities for 'collaboration between public and private providers and health-financing organizations', albeit under government stewardship (WHO 2005).

Paradoxically, that same year WHO established a Commission on Social Determinants of Health (CSDOH) to look into broader ways of addressing health inequity that transcended the health sector. Its report, presented in 2008, famously declared that 'social injustice is killing people on a grand scale', and contended that addressing health inequity (both between and within countries) was a matter of social justice. Issuing a series of recommendations that addressed living and work conditions, social protection, and the distribution of power and resources, the report also called for universal healthcare, specifically a single tier of healthcare financed through general taxation or mandatory insurance. It also drew attention to the pressing need to stem the health brain drain (WHO CSDOH 2008).

Also, in 2008, the WHR called for a system-wide whole-of-government approach based on WHO's Health in All Policies (HiAP) framework, which emphasised action beyond the health sector to advance health equity (WHO 2008a: xviii). Calling out 'structural adjustment, decentralization, blueprint poverty reduction strategies, insensitive trade policies, new tax regimes, fiscal policies and the withdrawal of the state' as 'hasty and disruptive interventions' (p. 9), the 2008 WHR decried the disparate standards guiding PHC reforms in LICs; in particular, the targeting of a handful of priority diseases and the narrowing of primary care to a standalone health post financed through out-of-pocket payments (WHO 2008a: xvii). But this would prove but a brief interregnum in the long post-Alma-Ata assault on public healthcare systems.

Indeed, the 2008 WHR introduced 'people-centred care', presented as an alternative to traditional 'command and control' (read state-centric) approaches to disease control. Whether a healthcare system was public or private mattered much less than its affordability, quality and 'people-centred[ness]' according to WHO (WHO 2008a). The notion of 'people-centred' healthcare served to blur the lines between public and private, and supported diversification of provision within 'pluralistic' or 'mixed' systems. It also effectively closed possibilities for the delivery of people-centred care within state-centric systems.

WHO launched the current formulation of UHC with a framework for implementation in the 2010 WHR (WHO 2010a). Identifying financial resource constraints, reliance on direct payments, and inefficient and inequitable use of healthcare resources as key impediments to UHC, the report proposed strategies for governments to 'fix' healthcare systems, primarily by: raising domestic funds for health, removing financial risk/barriers to access, eliminating waste, and improving efficiency (pp. xii–xviii). To harness domestic financial resources, WHO recommended that countries increase the efficiency of revenue collection, reprioritize government budgets, and engage in 'innovative' financing (e.g., taxes on financial transactions, air travel, tobacco, etc.). Although WHO appealed to donors to make available development assistance for health *for LICs*, the emphasis remained on generating domestic resources rather than international cooperation (pp. xii–xiii).

WHO framed the state's role in UHC primarily in relation to stewardship, encompassing oversight, regulation, and accountability of *both public and private sectors* (WHO 2014a). For instance, the 2010 WHR contained no mention of state involvement in healthcare delivery beyond 'ensur[ing] that all providers, public and private, operate appropriately and attend to patients' needs cost effectively and efficiently' (WHO 2010a: xviii). The 2008 WHR's language of social protection and universal access was missing from the 2010 report. That same year, WHA 63.27 resolved to '[strengthen] the capacity of governments to constructively engage with the private sector in providing essential health-care services' (WHO 2010b).

Although WHO defined pre-payment to include both tax- and insurance-driven pooling of funds, implicit in the 2010 report was a financing model based on health insurance. Atop the insistent use of 'coverage' (in lieu of access), the famed UHC cube depicts three dimensions, namely, population coverage, financial risk protection, and service comprehensiveness, upholding the notion of 'new universalism.' The dimensions of the smaller solid blue cube ('current pooled funds') placed at the centre of the UHC cube would depend on the extent to which a healthcare financing system maximized its reach (WHO 2010a, Figure 1). Notably, an earlier version of the cube that appeared in the 2008 WHR named the inner cube 'public expenditure on health' and used the explicit language of insurance (WHO 2008a, Figure 2).

The steady incursion of the private sector in the name of UHC has been masked by monitoring indicators that fail to distinguish between public and

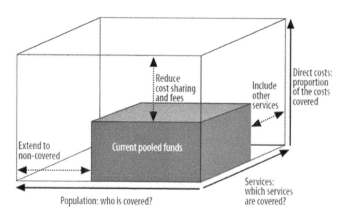

Figure 1 Dimensions to consider when moving towards universal coverage as depicted in the 2010 World Health Report (Reproduced with permission from WHO)

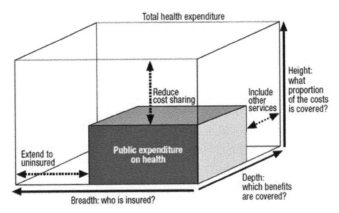

Figure 2 Three ways to move towards universal coverage as depicted in the 2008 World Health Report (Reproduced with permission from WHO)

private. The WHO and World Bank's (2014) UHC monitoring framework focused on health services coverage and financial risk protection for the prevention or treatment of specific diseases, with no distinction made regarding whether financing sources and delivery facilities were public or private. This erasure was based on the uncritical assumption that 'all health financing systems, regardless of the label attached' perform the same set of functions (WHO 2018a: 31). Today, neither the indicators of SDG 3's UHC target nor the numerous UHC coverage indices developed since, measure the extent of public or private involvement in healthcare financing and delivery (Lozano et al. 2020; WHO and World Bank 2021).

Even as global health policy directives blurred the distinction between public and private, the role and influence of the for-profit private health sector grew, catering to insured (better-off) households, while piecemeal interventions underpinned by social innovation became the name of the game in LICs (Section 3). Along these lines, the World Bank's (2016) Framework for Action on UHC in Africa called for innovative methods of financing and delivery, such as social health franchising and/or contracting health services. UHC2030, established in 2016, fuelled further corporatization, with its 'joint vision' calling for 'harnessing the investment capacity of the private sector' (p. 16), and detailing ways to make healthcare 'everybody's business' (p. 22). It made the spurious claim that achieving universal reach would require 'greater engagement and creative partnerships' (p. 14) with non-profit and for-profit non-state actors (WHO and World Bank 2017).

Still, rhetorical support for health equity emerged from the usual quarters. The 2018 Astana Declaration, marking the fortieth anniversary of Alma-Ata, reaffirmed a Health for All commitment, envisioning 'Primary health care and health services that are high quality, safe, comprehensive, integrated, accessible, available and affordable for everyone and everywhere' (WHO and UNICEF 2018). It emphasized multisectoral collaboration to address the social determinants of health, naming the private sector as a stakeholder. In an accompanying technical series, WHO (2018b) elaborated on the private sector's role in primary care and how private sector contributions can be channelled toward UHC. Likewise, the UN's 2019 Political Declaration of the High-level Meeting on Universal Health Coverage referenced the social determinants of health and recognized the importance of 'equity, social justice and social protection mechanisms' plus the need to '[eliminate] the root causes of discrimination and stigma in health-care settings'. Recalling the PHC vision embraced at Alma-Ata and Astana, the Political Declaration adopted a more expansive and inclusive definition of UHC, committing to '. . . people-centred, gender- and disability-responsive, and evidence-based interventions', delivered through the life course, particularly targeting those made vulnerable. Undergirded by this inclusive language, the UN also noted the role of private sector investment for UHC, and, in particular, recognized the private sector's role in developing health technologies and medicines.

In parallel, the Private Sector Constituency of UHC2030 detailed the role and reach of the private sector, including the for-profit sector – claimed to 'provide over 60% of health services in some countries'. The Constituency committed to '[d]evelop, test and scale up innovative business models' and '[c]reate, adapt, apply and scale up innovations' to assist governments to '"leapfrog" along health and development pathways' toward UHC. Describing how governments could create private-sector-enabling environments, the Constituency hailed public financing, urging governments to 'mobilise adequate and sustainable public financing' for PHC, as 'the foundation for *all stakeholders' contributions to UHC*' (UHC2030 n.d.a, emphasis added) underscoring the role of public financing in sustaining the private sector. By 2020, WHO too was calling for 'the meaningful inclusion of private providers for service delivery in mixed health systems' (WHO 2020a), based on the unquestioned premise that the private sector delivers a large share of services in some LMICs and therefore needed regulation. WHO proceeded to issue step-by-step technical guidance for governments on how exactly to engage the private sector, for instance, guidance on contracting for healthcare services during the Covid-19 pandemic (WHO 2020b).

In sum, UHC's advent signalled renewed attention to achieving universal healthcare, albeit premised on private sector involvement. Universal access was subsumed by the language of coverage within an insurance-based financing model. Despite rhetorical attention towards addressing inequity and the social determinants of health, the private sector's key UHC 'stakeholder' role derives from its foothold in the WHA 58.33 resolution, in turn shaped by decades of World Bank-led interventions in global health. Under growing corporate influence, today private sector engagement is a key pillar for action on UHC.

Conclusion

Despite its progressive underpinnings, a closer reading of Alma-Ata reveals the declaration's failure to call for a *single level* of comprehensive PHC for peoples across the world, portending subsequent developments. The ideological swing towards neoliberalism and healthcare user-fees that began in the 1980s, followed by the endorsement of an essential services package under evolving privatization regimes in the post–Cold War era, suggests that the current rendering of UHC has long been in the making, as have its imperatives for private sector engagement. Transformations in definitions and approaches to universal health/healthcare took place under a shifting constellation of actors at the helm, most prominently the World Bank, backed by prominent bilateral agencies, philanthropies, and PPPs, and supported by the UN and WHO. Today, actors of all stripes and orientations welcome UHC. While critical questions have been raised regarding UHC's implicit insurance-based financing model and explicit support for 'pluralistic' delivery, and its eluding of health promotion, disease prevention, and the social determinants of health (Global Health Watch 2017), less attention has been paid to the particularities of the practice and implementation of UHC in LICs – the topic of the next section.

3 Innovating for Whose Benefit? Global Health Inc.'s Ventures in Low-Income Settings

Corporate-backed primary care initiatives in low-income settings increasingly draw on a theory of change that has its basis in social innovation, defined by Phillis et al. (2008: 36) as 'a novel solution to a social problem that is more effective, efficient, sustainable, or just than existing solutions and for which the value created accrues primarily to society as a whole rather than private individuals'. Despite its purported goals, in practice, social innovation involves applying market principles and business models to social problems. As we demonstrate in this section, social innovation in global health has its basis in the model of 'catalytic innovation' proposed by Christensen and colleagues (2006) in the *Harvard*

Business Review. Underpinned by Christensen's (1997) prior work on 'disruptive innovation' conceived of to maximize profits through industry capture, the catalytic model offers more 'efficient' (read cheaper and lower quality) alternatives that target less demanding consumers in lower-end niche markets in pursuance of social goals (Christensen et al. 2006: 1–2).

Today, social innovation is an interdisciplinary endeavour supported by a slew of academic centres – many in business schools – handsomely supported by a range of actors, including the World Economic Forum (see Duke Innovation and Entrepreneurship 2022; Said Business School 2023; Stanford Graduate School of Business n.d.). Social innovation's headway in global health is evidenced in its incursion and uptake by WHO and its promotion by other global health agencies, including and especially BMGF (Global Grand Challenges 2003–23; Halpaap et al. 2020). The Social Innovations in Health Initiative (SIHI) was launched in 2014 as a collaboration among UNICEF, UNDP, the World Bank and WHO – which jointly co-sponsor TDR – and several academic centres (Halpaap et al. 2019). It is a prime illustration of the mounting presence of private sector actors and values in global health.

For SIHI, social innovations are locally grown solutions that provide 'creative and unconventional approaches' to fixing the world's most 'complex and wicked problems' (TDR 2021). Through social innovation, SIHI contends, countries can work towards building 'sustainable, equitable, and integrated people-centred health systems' in view of UHC (TDR 2021). To learn from and disseminate knowledge on social innovations in health, SIHI has carried out forty-plus case studies, identified through crowdsourcing calls to generate ideas for scale-up, from across Africa, Asia, Latin America, and the Caribbean. Rolled out especially in communities subject to conditions of extreme poverty, these innovations target primary care, mainly maternal and child health.

This section delves into three SIHI case studies of social innovation, to critically examine what this approach means for PHC in underserved areas of the Majority World. The case studies, drawn from three LICs according to World Bank tallies, illustrate different modalities of innovation, all of them 'multi-stakeholder initiatives' involving diverse actors, including international and local NGOs, universities, and the private sector, located in and outside the respective countries, working alongside governments as PPPs. They include a hotline and mobile messaging service to improve maternal and child health literacy and health seeking behaviour in rural Malawi; an effort to engage private drug shops in rural Uganda for the treatment of childhood fever; and a franchise in rural Rwanda that places independent 'nurse entrepreneurs' in rural outposts to deliver primary care. We selected the three projects in tandem with the PHC systems in Section 4 to illustrate the contrasting approaches taken in the different settings to PHC. Having said that, a quick perusal of the SIHI website would confirm that they are quite typical of social innovations in global health (see TDR 2021). That all three innovations were piloted or implemented in the Sub-Saharan African region reflects the location of most SIHI case studies (TDR 2021), and much social innovations in health work more broadly.

We begin each case with a project description, then provide deeper contextualization, and conclude with a critical analysis of the extent to which the 'innovation' addresses leading healthcare concerns in the specific region. We foreground the project rather than the social, political, or economic context because our intention is to highlight the nature of the innovation and its mismatch to the healthcare setting. We do not in any way intend to discredit the work being carried out by well-meaning individuals or organizations; rather, we apply a critical political economy of health framing to examine how social innovation is being co-opted by Global Health Inc. to ultimately arrive at a narrow, corporatized form of primary care. We suggest that this insidious form of corporatization opens new hard-to-reach markets to global health TNCs writ large, furthering dispossession in the Majority World.

Mhealth Technologies for Maternal and Child Health

Chipatala Cha Pa Foni (CCPF), meaning 'Health Centre by Phone', is a toll-free health hotline and mobile messaging service designed to increase access to health information and improve healthcare seeking among underserved communities in rural Malawi. The hotline connects people in rural areas with trained volunteers who provide health advice or direct users to healthcare facilities, if needed. The information provided is based on mobile health (mhealth) protocols developed to align with Ministry of Health guidelines, and is backed by support from nurses (and doctors) when needed. The text/voice messaging service sends out weekly health messages tailored to specific groups, including pregnant and postpartum women, adolescents, and so on. The touchscreen mobile platform used by service providers purports to facilitate monitoring and evaluation. Originally designed to improve maternal, newborn, and child health, CCPF's scope has since expanded to other areas, including nutrition, HIV prevention, adolescent health, and personal hygiene (Blauvelt et al. 2018; Castillo and Vosloo 2017).

The CCPF concept was developed by 'innovators' in Uganda through the 'Share an idea, save a life' campaign funded by Concern Worldwide – a humanitarian organization set up in the 1960s to provide food aid during the Biafran war – under its Innovations for Maternal, Newborn and Child Health programme funded by BMGF (Maurrasse 2021). The project was first rolled out in Balaka, a rural district of Malawi, in 2011, as a partnership led by

VillageReach, a Seattle-based non-profit, with the Government of Malawi. The technology for CCPF was developed by the Baobab Health Trust, a local NGO, Yo! Uganda, a technology solutions company, and VillageReach. Airtel, a telecommunications TNC, joined the partnership in 2015 to offer telecommunications support and cover the cost of incoming calls and the messaging service. Follow-up calls, provided at a discounted rate by Airtel, were initially funded by VillageReach. The project was scaled up with a catalytic mhealth grant from the UN Innovation Working Group hosted by WHO's Partnership for Maternal, Newborn and Child Health (Blauvelt et al. 2018; UN Foundation et al. n.d.; WHO 2014b). More recently, CCPF has been supported by the United States President's Emergency Plan for AIDS Relief (PEPFAR) through its DREAMS Innovation Challenge, and USAID's Organized Network of Services for Everyone's Health Activity. Since 2018, the hotline is available across Malawi to all those with access to an Airtel phone (Blauvelt et al. 2018). In 2020, Malawi's National Planning Commission recognized CCPF as a 'transformative initiative for the country' (VillageReach 2020a); two years later VillageReach was in the process of handing over CCPF to the Malawian Ministry of Health (VillageReach 2022).

Internal and external evaluations of CCPF have documented improvements in health behaviour. A 2013 external evaluation by the Malawi-based Invest in Knowledge Initiative noted that CCPF users reported higher rates of prenatal care use in the first trimester, earlier initiation of breastfeeding, and greater use of bed nets, compared to non-users (Watkins et al. 2013). A 2018 internal evaluation also documented better knowledge, lower rates of unplanned pregnancy, and greater use of bed nets, contraceptives, prenatal care, HIV testing, and vaccination among CCPF users (VillageReach 2020b). However, by 2018, seven years after the project's launch, only 0.3 per cent of the Malawian population used CCPF, and one-quarter of CCPF users did not have direct access to a(n) (Airtel) mobile phone, instead relying on community volunteers, family or friends to connect them to the service (Blauvelt et al. 2018; VillageReach 2020b). Funding constraints and greater demand have led to higher wait-times to speak with a service provider (Blauvelt et al. 2018). Apart from these challenges, a larger question remains unanswered: To what extent does CCPF contribute towards preventing maternal and infant mortality in rural Malawi?

Chipatala Cha Pa Foni in Context

Malawi is among the twenty lowest-income countries in the world, according to the World Bank (GDP per capita (current USD) USD 635 in 2021). The country's population is approximately 20 million, with about 80 per cent residing in rural areas, many without access to basic needs. In 2020, 33 per cent of the rural population did not use basic drinking water services, while 75 per cent and 93 per cent of rural dwellers had no access to basic sanitary facilities and electricity, respectively. Over a third (36 per cent in 2021) of adult females over fifteen years cannot read or write, and the country reports high rates of maternal, newborn, infant, and child mortality, and HIV. In 2017, Malawi's maternal mortality ratio was 350 deaths per 100,000 live births (World Bank 2023), contributing over 2,000 deaths to the global yearly total of approximately 300,000 maternal deaths (WHO n.d.).

The healthcare system of Malawi consists of a mix of public, non-profit, and for-profit facilities. Some two-thirds of healthcare services are delivered by the government with no user charges at points of delivery; roughly a quarter are purveyed by the non-profit Christian Health Association of Malawi (CHAM), the main provider in rural areas. CHAM offers services for a nominal fee (although charges can be prohibitive relative to income); under its UHC policy, the government covers an essential services package through CHAM facilities, but in practice the shortfall of services compels people to consult private providers (Chansa and Pattnaik 2018; Masefield et al. 2020). A much smaller share of services (less than 10 per cent) concentrated in urban areas is delivered by the for-profit private sector (Masefield et al. 2020). The government allocates about 9 per cent of its budget to health, which translates to (current) USD 10 per capita, accounting for about a third of current health expenditures. Over 40 per cent of health spending is sourced from donors, with private financing contributing to just under a quarter, much of it out-of-pocket (17 per cent) (World Bank 2023).

Chronically low levels of funding have hobbled Malawi's healthcare system. Healthcare facilities are understaffed, with staff vacancy rates as high as 50 per cent, according to some estimates (Masefield et al. 2020). The country reports <0.1 physicians and 0.4 nurses/midwives per 1,000 population, compared with 3.8 and 10.4 per 1,000 population in OECD countries (World Bank 2023). Health facilities lack vital requirements, including beds, and report widespread shortages of pharmaceuticals, equipment, and basic medical supplies, particularly in rural areas. Rural public transport is virtually non-existent and road connectivity is poor, requiring people to trek long distances or use unsafe transport to reach care (Chansa and Pattnaik 2018; Masefield et al. 2020).

The use of prenatal care is quite high (94 per cent), although only roughly half of pregnant women record four or more visits (Government of Malawi 2016). Community health workers deliver a basic maternal and newborn care package in selected districts (Guenther et al. 2019), but a dearth of facilities impedes access to basic obstetric care, compounded by a woefully inadequate number of specialists, and a dysfunctional ambulance service. Although 90 per cent of births take place at health facilities, mostly at health centres, accessing hospital care during an obstetric emergency involves considerable travel, and remains challenging at many levels (Machira and Palamuleni 2017, 2018). A 2016 study carried out in Mangochi, Malawi, linked maternal mortality to gaps in health-care access and quality; of 151 maternal deaths identified during a twelve-month period, 57 (38 per cent) women died at home, of whom 25 did not seek care owing to poverty, distance to healthcare or prior negative healthcare experiences (Mgawadere et al. 2017).

Limits of Mhealth Approaches

Even as thousands of women die during childbirth in deprived social conditions without access to emergency obstetric care, VillageReach, CCPF's creator, asserts that in Malawi 'knowing where and when to seek care' is crucial (VillageReach n.d.). Thus, the Seattle-based non-profit justifies its technology-based innovation focus on 'empowering' women with information, without intervening on the infrastructural and health worker impediments or conditions of extreme poverty that so fundamentally contribute to maternal mortality in rural Malawi.

The women's stories posted on the VillageReach website are telling. Consider Mercy, a twenty-four-year-old pregnant woman who travelled 12 km to the nearest health centre on the back of a neighbour's bicycle, and went into labour on the way. CCPF arranged an ambulance, which arrived after the delivery, and transported Mercy, now bleeding heavily, for life-saving obstetric care (VillageReach 2013). Hawa, twenty years old, called CCPF regarding an unrepaired fistula – after having suffered through prolonged labour and a stillbirth 100 miles from the closest hospital, three years prior. CCPF arranged for Hawa to travel to a distant facility where she was treated successfully by the only urologist in the country (VillageReach 2016). Although CCPF undoubtedly made a difference in these women's lives by delivering information and coordinating care, very little changed 'on the ground' in terms of the availability of maternity care in rural Malawi.

Neglected by governments and the global health community, women continue to get very sick or die during childbirth without access to appropriate care. Even within the narrow mandate of a hotline and messaging service, less than 1 per cent of the Malawian population uses CCPF (Blauvelt et al. 2018), and those who do connect with a trained community volunteer (now called a health worker) receive health information (Breakthrough REACH and VillageReach 2021). In reality, CCPF does not address crucial gaps in Malawi's rural health system. Nevertheless, global health agencies, and various other actors hail CCPF as a resounding success, citing improvements in health behaviours and savings on time and transport (Blauvelt et al. 2018; Halpaap et al. 2020).

As dominant actors in global health call for CCPF's 'scale-up' and expansion to underserved rural areas in other countries, other stakeholders, especially corporate actors, stand to gain. According to the 2018 CCPF evaluation, 77 per cent of CCPF users in the project implementation area owned an Airtel phone, up from about a quarter in 2013 (VillageReach 2020b). Airtel's CSR initiative appears to have fruitfully served the company's tacit aim of expanding its market to countries across the African continent. Furthermore, non-profits like VillageReach, mostly based in the global North, continue to receive millions of tax-exempt dollars to roll out mhealth projects, which require large investments in digital technologies, with the profits going to corporate entities (Al Dahdah 2022). These precious funds could instead be channelled toward strengthening Malawi's public healthcare system so that it has the capacity to serve 'hard to reach' communities in rural areas.

Private Drug Sellers Treating Childhood Fever

Led by researchers at Makerere University, a project was launched in 2011 to explore the feasibility of engaging private drug sellers to improve access to primary care for three febrile illnesses – malaria, pneumonia, and non-bloody diarrhoea – among children under five in rural Uganda (van Niekerk and Chater 2016a). Private drug shops in Uganda are mostly owner-run; many drug sellers have no formal pharmacy training yet function as first points of care in rural villages (Awor et al. 2012). The project came on the heels of the Ugandan Ministry of Health's 2010 adoption of the integrated community case management (iCCM) strategy – involving training and supporting lay community members to treat childhood fever (WHO/UNICEF 2012). At present, over 100,000 community volunteers serve in village health teams delivering iCCM under the Ministry of Health (Awor et al. 2022).

A collaboration among Makerere University and three Scandinavian universities (Karolinska Institute, Uppsala University, and University of Bergen), the project was initially piloted in Kaliro District, Eastern Uganda. It involved delivering a 5-day training programme on iCCM to drug sellers, along with supplies of rapid diagnostic test kits (RDT, for malaria), respiratory timers (for pneumonia), and packed units of artemisinin-based combination therapy

(ACT, for malaria), oral rehydration salts (ORS) and zinc sulphate (for diar-rhoea), and amoxicillin (for pneumonia). The Ministry of Health authorised participating drug sellers to manage the three febrile illnesses, and refer patients to public healthcare facilities when needed. The service package included health advice and diagnostics on a non-fee levying basis, and (project-subsidized) medicines sold with a profit margin of 50 per cent to 80 per cent to generate income for the drug shops. As per the iCCM protocol, a community-level campaign was carried out to raise awareness of the revamped services and supplies available at the drug shops. The project was scaled up in 2013 to Mbarara District, Western Uganda with TDR funding and support from the Einhorn Family Foundation, Swedish Research Council, Medicines for Malaria Venture, WHO and Grand Challenges Canada (Awor et al. 2014; van Niekerk and Chater 2016a).

Evaluations by the project team suggest that the intervention led to an increase in use of diagnostics, with accompanying declines in antimicrobial use. A quasi-experimental study that compared the situation in an intervention district against a non-intervention district found that a substantial proportion of children with fever (88 per cent) and cough with difficulty in breathing (55 per cent) were investigated with a malaria RDT or respiratory timer as relevant, compared to zero children in the non-intervention district. Although children in the intervention district were approximately thirteen times more likely to be treated with ORS/zinc sulphate, and three and four times more likely to be treated with amoxicillin and ACT respectively, an 18 per cent decline in overall antimicrobial use was reported in the intervention group (Awor et al. 2014). This was perhaps because the use of RDT to diagnose malaria led to a fall in the prescription of antimalarials (Kitutu et al. 2017).

Despite concerns expressed by the Ministry of Health regarding the possibil-ity of over-prescription (and resulting antimicrobial resistance), and the drug shops' revenue being linked to the sale of medicines, post-intervention studies showed improved adherence to treatment protocols (Awor et al. 2015). Yet medical professionals remain apprehensive about the engagement of (trained) community volunteers for iCCM, given their limited level of education (Awor et al. 2022). Comparisons of iCCM by community workers, as per the Ministry of Health protocol, versus that delivered by private drug sellers found that they were similarly 'cost-effective', although the latter incurred savings for the government by transferring some costs to households (Lubogo et al. 2021). At present, the Ministry of Health's iCCM programme delivered by community volunteers/health workers continues amid dire funding constraints, and private drug shops are still not formally engaged by the Ugandan Ministry of Health for iCCM (Awor et al. 2021).

Private Drug Shops in Context

Uganda is home to a population of roughly 46 million people. In 2021, per capita GDP was (current) USD 884. About a quarter (26 per cent in 2021) of females over fifteen years cannot read or write and approximately three-quarters of the population lives in rural areas, where many do not have access to basic facilities. In 2020, over half (52 per cent) of the rural population did not use basic drinking water services, while 83 per cent and 67 per cent had no access to sanitary facilities and household electricity, respectively. Like Malawi, Uganda records high levels of maternal, newborn, infant, and child mortality, and HIV (World Bank 2023).

The Ugandan healthcare system is made up of public facilities, non-profit (mostly faith-based) health centres, for-profit health centres, and some for-profit hospitals (ThinkWell 2020). A 2010 mapping study of three rural districts found that only 19 (4 per cent) of a total of 445 healthcare facilities were publicly owned, namely one hospital and eighteen health centres. The private sector (96 per cent) comprised 7 non-profit health centres, 76 for-profit health centres (including registered drug shops), 43 shops that sold medicines along with other merchandise, and 300 traditional practitioners (Konde-Lule et al. 2010). At present, about 3 per cent of the budget is allocated to health, translating to a per capita government health expenditure of (current) USD 5. In 2019, the public contribution to current health expenditure was 15 per cent of the total, the major share being privately financed (43 per cent) – mainly by households (38 per cent) – or externally sourced (42 per cent) (World Bank 2023). Although government facilities are non-fee levying, much of rural health service delivery takes place in the private sector, resulting in substantial out-of-pocket expenses (Kwesiga et al. 2020).

Favoured by PEPFAR, Uganda's health sector has received substantial funding and technical support from the US government since 2005 for the development of HIV services, albeit with a slew of neoliberal conditionalities. The healthcare system did experience certain infrastructural advantages in subsequent decades, but the vertical design of this support and the preference for largely faith-based NGOs for service provision weakened non-HIV-related public healthcare (Lohman et al. 2017; Luboga et al. 2016). Today, bed shortages and deficits in equipment and other essentials are widely reported in the healthcare system (Birungi et al. 2001), staffed by just 0.2 physicians and 1.2 nurses/midwives per 1,000 population (World Bank 2023). Budget constraints impede recruitment of health workers to public facilities, resulting in long wait-times and suboptimal care. Under these circumstances, a sizeable proportion of the population, close to half according to some estimates, resorts to self-medication or foregoes healthcare, while the remainder use private providers, who are closer at hand (Konde-Lule et al. 2010). Located in rural villages, private drug shops are commonly accessed for primary care, including for febrile illnesses among children (Awor et al. 2012).

Limits of iCCM and Private Drug Sellers

In 2012, WHO and UNICEF introduced iCCM as a strategy to curb child mortality (WHO/UNICEF 2012); by 2020, however, they recommended that iCCM be integrated into a comprehensive service package for children, rather than a standalone programme (WHO/UNICEF 2020). The two multilateral organizations conceded that children needed better care than what was purveyed via iCCM, including 'immunization, adequate nutrition, safe water and food, and quality care by a trained health provider', all crucial for child survival and well-being (WHO 2020c).

Notwithstanding this shift in WHO's and UNICEF's position on iCCM, the Ugandan private drug shop project has received wide acclaim (TDR 2017). Ironically, the 'innovative' element appears to centre on the private drug shops themselves, which are presented as an alternative to public sector health centres that are fewer in number, under-resourced and characterized by long wait-times and frequent stockouts. Yet private drug sellers seem to perform no better and are marred by knowledge gaps, rampant over-prescribing, and low overall standards (Mbonye et al. 2016). Many drug shops are unregistered, poorly supervised, and operated by providers with little or no pharmacy training (Mayora et al. 2018), risking potentially ineffective or harmful prescribing practices (Bagonza et al. 2020). Most importantly, private drug shops are fee-levying, unlike public health centres.

The sustainability of this venture, from the point of view of donors, pivots on the charges levied on users. Private drug sellers, once integrated into the healthcare system, would remain self-sustaining, and not on the government's payroll. Although the project subsidized diagnostic and medical supplies, private drug shops charged households for medicines – at about USD 0.38 per unit, a substantial sum in Uganda where per capita government health expenditure is a mere USD 5. The Ministry of Health's current iCCM programme delivers the same service package on a non-fee-levying basis, although problematically relying on unpaid community volunteers (Awor et al. 2014). The fee-sustaining private drug shop programme, if scaled up nationally, would likely deter families with little or no income from accessing care. It also remains unclear as to how drug sellers will be held accountable once responsibility, previously the government's, is relocated to private drug shops. Nonetheless, this approach would appeal to a debt-ridden LIC government, as the Ministry of Health would not need to cover overheads, supplies, or salaries.

Private drug shops grossly inadequately heed UHC's (avowedly limited) call for universal essential and affordable quality healthcare services. Beyond concerns around affordability (for users), this project (and iCCM generally) has highly circumscribed aims, seeking to improve access to just two diagnostic tests and three treatments. That these services are delivered through drug shop sellers who mostly have only minimal or no pharmacy training, called 'task shifting', also raises serious quality concerns. Ultimately, the project does little to strengthen the Ugandan healthcare system, whether by investing in health infrastructure, training health workers, or addressing quality of care. The social determinants of health, such as nutrition and safe water/sanitation, identified by WHO and UNICEF as crucial for child survival, are similarly left out.

Franchisee-Nurses Delivering Primary Care

One Family Health Rwanda (OFHR) is a low-profit limited liability franchising company[4] of the US-based One Family Health Foundation. OFHR was launched in 2012 to extend primary care to rural, mountainous regions of Rwanda. Nurses at a lower tier of training and experience are recruited to work for the franchise as independent 'nurse entrepreneurs' providing a standardized package of primary care services at rural outposts (van Niekerk and Chater 2016b). OFHR functions as a PPP partnered with the Government of Rwanda; the government funds OFHR services for individuals enrolled in Rwanda's mandatory (but not universal)[5] community-based health insurance (CBHI) scheme (details ahead). At present, over 100 OFHR posts, linked to public facilities via a referral system, operate in 14 of Rwanda's 30 districts, serving a population of 1.6 million, about 15 per cent of Rwanda's population (Kalapurakkel 2021; OFH n.d.).

Established by Gunther Faber, former Vice President for GSK Sub-Saharan Africa, the OFH Foundation's current funders include three pharmaceutical TNCs (GSK, Pfizer, and UCB) and USAID (OFH n.d.; van Niekerk and Chater 2016b). OFHR was set up with an interest-free 'loan' from GSK, in reality a grant repayable to Rwanda's Ministry of Health once the company incurs profit. OFHR generates revenue from franchise royalty fees paid by

---

[4] A low-profit limited liability company, under US law, refers to a legal entity 'designed to attract private investments and philanthropic capital' in ventures that have a primarily social mission; they have both non-profit and for-profit attributes and may distribute their profits to shareholders (Glackin, n.d.).

[5] In 2018, 82 per cent of the Rwandan population were covered by CBHI, and another 6 per cent covered by other schemes. A section of the poor remains uncovered as they do not qualify for government subsidization and cannot afford to pay the premiums (Chemouni, 2018).

nurses (6 per cent of monthly earnings) and a 5 per cent profit margin from sales of medicines, plus an additional 3 per cent margin on distribution of medicines to the rural posts. Nurses must also pay a USD 500 fee to enter the franchise, and direct a further 2 per cent of monthly earnings to marketing (van Niekerk and Chater 2016b). While these profit tithes, royalties, and other fees are characteristic of low-profit companies, they represent sizeable obligations on the part of both nurses and healthcare users.

OFHR offers low-interest loans, financed by EcoBank – a pan-African banking conglomerate – to its franchisees for the purchase of clinic equipment and medical supplies, repayable over a 5-year period. The government permits free-for-now use of public lands and buildings to set up health posts. OFHR trains the nurses in primary care protocols through an open-source platform, available via a basic mobile phone with internet connectivity. In addition, all nurses must undergo one-week's training at a high-performing OFHR post. OFHR delivers medicines to health posts, supervised by district OFHR personnel, ensuring continuous supplies. Its mobile platform is expected to aid monitoring and evaluation, delivery of medical supplies, and the processing of insurance claims (Charles et al. 2013; Doshi et al. 2021; van Niekerk and Chater 2016b).

The 'nurse entrepreneurs' generate income through insurance reimbursements and patient co-payments. In 2015, Rwandans enrolled in the CBHI scheme paid USD 1.20 to 1.50 out-of-pocket per consultation at a rural post; those without coverage paid USD 2 to 4, plus a USD 0.30 co-payment. Each OFHR post, according to 2015 estimates, was expected to earn over USD 10,000 annually assuming twenty consultations per day, after deducting remuneration of assistants, expenses on medicines, and overhead costs (van Niekerk and Chater 2016b). According to a Duke Global Health analysis, at least 60 per cent of OFHR posts were 'profitable or sustainable' (Doshi et al. 2021: 8), although USAID and other donors were still OFHR's primary funders (Kalapurakkel 2021). Duke Global Health ranked the innovation high on sustainability because the nurses support themselves, accruing savings to the Ministry of Health of USD 3,600 per nurse per year. Once scaled up to 500 posts, it is expected to save the government up to 15 per cent of its health budget (Doshi et al. 2021).

An independent review of Rwanda's CBHI revealed that service utilization at OFHR health posts was greater than at other CBHI health posts (Emmanuel 2019), perhaps due to greater consistency of medicine supplies at OFHR posts (van Niekerk and Chater 2016b). A 2015 OFHR-commissioned evaluation found that the average travel time to healthcare facilities fell from seventy-four to fourteen minutes for communities served by OFHR, and that the latter offered shorter wait-times, better continuity of care, and integrated health promotion and disease prevention (Kalapurakkel 2021; van Niekerk and Chater 2016b). However, OFHR experiences ongoing challenges, including impediments with insurance disbursements, interruptions in water, electricity, and medicine supplies (still better than government posts), and referral bottlenecks (Kalapurakkel 2021).

One Family Health Rwanda in Context

Rwanda is a low-income country (GDP per capita (current) USD 822 in 2021) of about 13 million people, over 80 per cent of whom reside in rural areas. Over a quarter (27 per cent in 2021) of females over fifteen years cannot read or write, and about a half and a quarter of the rural population have no access to basic drinking water and sanitation facilities, while about 60 per cent have no household electricity. Rwanda's maternal, infant, and child mortality, and HIV prevalence are lower than in Malawi and Uganda but remain much higher than LMIC averages (World Bank 2023).

Rwanda spends approximately 9 per cent of its budget on health, translating to a per capita government expenditure on health of USD 21 – twice and four times that of Malawi and Uganda, respectively. In 2019, the government financed 40 per cent of health spending, and 34 per cent came from donors; private financing accounted for 26 per cent, made up of out-of-pocket payments (12 per cent) and CBHI contributions (World Bank 2023). Over 80 per cent of the population is covered by the mandatory CBHI scheme, which requires households to purchase premiums. Although the government subsidizes premiums and co-payments for the bottom income quartile, mechanisms to identify the poorest are complex and trouble-laden. Furthermore, to be eligible for coverage, all household members must pay the premium, making enrolment difficult for those unsubsidized (Chemouni 2018; Ridde et al. 2018). Noteworthy is that the CBHI scheme runs on a huge deficit, delaying disbursements, including to OFHR posts (Ministry of Health Rwanda 2018; van Niekerk and Chater 2016b).

Healthcare services in Rwanda are mostly public and delivered through tiered facilities. In 2017, the public sector comprised 45,000 plus community health workers, 470 health posts, 499 health centres, 36 district hospitals, 4 provincial hospitals, and 8 teaching hospitals (Ministry of Health Rwanda 2018). The health posts and centres deliver immunization, family planning, growth monitoring, prenatal care, and basic curative care (Kalapurakkel 2021). Health personnel at the centres supervise the rural posts and the activities of community health workers (Ministry of Health Rwanda 2018). The private sector, in 2015, consisted of 177 for-profit facilities (hospitals, polyclinics, clinic dispensaries) and 216 pharmacies and wholesalers (USAID 2015). With high attrition rates, the public healthcare system has an acute shortage of health workers (Odhiambo et al. 2017). In 2019, there were 0.1 physicians and 0.9 nurses/midwives per 1,000 population (World Bank 2023).

The use of primary care in rural areas is reportedly high; 95 per cent of children under 2 years receive basic vaccinations, about 98 per cent of women receive prenatal care, and over 90 per cent of deliveries take place with skilled assistance at health facilities (National Institute of Statistics of Rwanda and ICF 2020). However, these services are located at a distance, and public transport is patchy; long wait-times, opportunity costs, and unaffordable insurance premiums also impede access to healthcare (Holmlund et al. 2017).

Limits of Franchising for Primary Care

The public healthcare system is the dominant provider of primary care in Rwanda, financed chiefly via CBHI. Even so, access is difficult for communities living in remote mountainous regions where road connectivity is poor (Chemouni 2018; Tuyisenge et al. 2019). It is puzzling that OFHR franchising was identified as the solution for primary care gaps in these regions, in lieu of expanding the existing primary care system. Despite OFHR being credited as an innovation (van Niekerk and Chater 2016b), having nurse practitioners serve in hard-to-reach areas is hardly novel (Xue et al. 2019). What is 'innovative' here is that nurses at a lower tier of training ('task shifting') become self-sustaining entrepreneurs who run their health posts as businesses.

As with other social innovations, OFHR draws from a narrowly-defined vision of UHC, and not comprehensive PHC as articulated at Alma-Ata. Even when considered through a UHC lens, the 'package' does not include certain basic elements like maternity care (van Niekerk and Chater 2016b). Needless to say, the innovation does not advance action on environmental and other health determinants. Moreover, out-of-pocket payments (including co-payments), seemingly nominal in dollar terms, represent substantial barriers in Rwanda, where over half the population lives in poverty. The 'sustainability' of this project hinges upon the CBHI scheme, financed by households, government, donors, and cross-subsidization through other schemes (Chemouni 2018). Indeed, SIHI contends that a national health insurance scheme is key for OFHR scale-up (van Niekerk and Chater 2016b), suggesting that entrepreneurial ventures of this nature require state backing for their success.

OFHR is essentially a commercial enterprise (USAID 2015). Among the four (all white) One Family Health Foundation Board of Directors members, three are linked to Big Pharma or other business interests (One Family Health n.d.). On one hand, CBHI disbursements, co-payments, and out-of-pocket payments generate income for nurses; on the other, nurses themselves are key to OFHR's revenue generation, via franchise royalty fees, profit cuts on medicines and supplies distribution, and the USD 500 franchise entry fee. Although registered as a low-profit company, OFHR, like other social franchises, is poised to profit, with substantially less business risk given their PPP modus operandi. The Rwandan government finances services through CBHI and authorizes the use of public infrastructure, while franchisees – whose revenue is sourced from insurance disbursements and out-of-pocket expenses – shoulder overheads and other recurrent expenses. Primary care franchising could also fragment health systems into myriad of disconnected commercial enterprises, paving the way for further corporatization of healthcare.

Innovations for Profit not for People

As conceived and evaluated, the innovations examined here appear to be achieving their self-styled objectives, even as the evaluations tend to rely on internal reporting. Still, the innovations themselves entail narrowly-defined packages of primary care services that do not address systemic and structural healthcare access issues and rely primarily on exploiting women's (unpaid or poorly paid) care work. Despite using the language of equity, inclusion, and universalism, they do little to further social-justice-oriented PHC goals, instead reinforcing structural inequalities and promoting pro-corporate solutions in healthcare.

One might argue that these contextual limitations are inherent to any low-resource setting and that this section's selection of case studies – three Sub-Saharan African countries with among the world's lowest Human Development Index rankings (UNDP 2022) – perforce precludes the possibility of structural healthcare system transformation without socio-economic development. Yet it is precisely in such settings that Global Health Inc. is keen to expand – what are called 'fragile' settings where lower expectations of state accountability stemming from centuries of oppression and resource theft under colonial rule, extended in the current era of global extractivism characterized by illicit financial outflows, and military and economic repression, lubricate the entry of profit-seeking arrangements. Rather than addressing these constraints, social innovation approaches seek to seduce people and governments into pursuing an ever-evolving menu of narrow market-based solutions to gargantuan political economy challenges without ever addressing larger structural issues.

That these innovations are flawed from their very design – involving piece-meal interventions of dubious quality, inexperienced health workers, onerous user charges, narrow targets/ evaluations, insufficient funding except in the case of funding entrepreneurs, reliance on purchasing TNC products, niche markets, minimal health infrastructure investment, robbery of public sector resources – only serves as justification for a never-ending parade of market-oriented inter-ventions to fix the last failure. Yet as we explore in Section 4, such limitations are not inevitable. Indeed, the three country experiences we examine historic-ally faced many of the same constraints as Malawi, Uganda, and Rwanda, but claims on the state and persistent resistance spurred remarkable transformative change that unfolded over time.

Indubitably, the social innovations approach is characterized by neoliberal thinking; applied to the UHC goal, it holds that: (1) innovators can solve the world's most knotty problems, detached from social context, if only provided sufficient incentives and opportunities to do so; and (2) business solutions work when entrepreneurs are supported to develop their ideas, unimpeded by ineffi-cient state bureaucracies and machinery (Pfotenhauer and Juhl 2017). To note, none of the innovations examined here were designed within ministries of health, arguably best-placed to gauge the potential effectiveness and utility of health programmes. At the same time, all three adopted business models to deliver low-cost technologies, involving task shifting, and targeting niche markets for lower-quality services, closely heeding the model of catalytic innovations (Christensen et al. 2006). Although technology transfer has been integral to the UN's development cooperation agenda for decades, today's corporatized formulae seek to expand markets for largely untested technologies in the Majority World (Fejerskov 2017).

Even within the lamentably circumscribed definition of UHC, where health is framed in terms of some services covered by insurance, and the social determin-ants of health are neglected, UHC is a huge undertaking, requiring massive state investment (Dieleman et al. 2018). Rather than looking to governments to build strong healthcare systems, however, the mainstream global health community pursues the kinds of social innovation depicted in this section, typically imple-mented by non-state actors who often engage with the for-profit private sector. Certainly, the language of innovation has long been used to delegitimize and overturn conventional forms of welfare (Moulaert et al. 2013). Social innovations in health solutions that 'cut across traditional silos and sit outside the traditional boxes' (TDR 2021) and '[disrupt] established systems of health service delivery' (Halpaap 2020: e633) likewise fit this mould.

The creed that private sector engagement is central to social policy success, widely championed by the World Bank, WHO, and corporate actors, has encouraged UHC projects that invite private providers into healthcare systems. Social innovations, while involving non-profits, for-profits and private philanthropies rely extensively on CSR or donors for financing health technologies and products. However, state subsidies – public infrastructure, in-kind support, financing – remain integral to their success. For OFHR, for instance, the CBHI scheme guarantees an income for 'nurse entrepreneurs' and, in fact, necessitates national health insurance scheme financing for scale-up in other countries (van Niekerk and Chater 2016b).

The expectation of sustainability – a misnomer of sorts for cost recovery – is fundamental not just to social innovation but also to UHC. People must purchase mobile phones, pay for subsidized medicines, or spend on co-payments or user-fees in order to benefit from the innovations. Yet amid widespread poverty, the very 'sustainability', not to mention the ethics, of these ventures is highly questionable. Even so, innovations do directly and indirectly 'sustain' a range of other stakeholders, including non-profits, universities, and for-profit companies. Private philanthropies along with the non-profits they support, receive tax exemptions, even as they fund for-profit companies – mostly based in the global North – to develop health technologies (Al Dahdah 2022); likewise, granting agencies reward universities and researchers for promulgating 'sustainability' and 'cost-effectiveness' in their projects.

Despite the language of bottom-up solutions and community participation, most social innovation projects are neither designed nor implemented by the communities they purport to serve (see TDR 2021). The CCPF project was designed by VillageReach, a US-based non-profit with input from a 'local' NGO and tech company; OFHR is an extension of a US foundation, also registered as a company in Rwanda. Such arrangements are consistent with the larger global health enterprise, whereby researchers and consultants whiz back and forth between North America/Europe and the Majority World, reflecting the power asymmetries in global health and the legacies of colonial medicine and top-down international health (Birn et al. 2017). That a sizeable proportion of health financing (over a third in our examples) is sourced externally also facilitates donor involvement in priority-setting and programme development.

Focused on health technologies, social innovations are undergirded by leading global health actors, their interests, and ideologies. Under the rubric of mhealth, CCPF emerged from an initiative funded by BMGF, established by business magnate-turned-philanthropist Bill Gates (and ex-wife Melinda), whose wealth derives from the information technology industry. The private drug shops project builds on the Affordable Medicines Facility for Malaria (AMFm), initially piloted in 2008 by the Global Fund, in turn supported by BMGF, to improve the availability and quality of ACT in LICs by engaging the private sector. AMFm offered buyer subsidies to drug manufacturers, resulting in lower prices for first-line purchasers (both governments and private entities) theoretically passed on to pharmacies and consumers, to push obsolete mono-therapies off the market (Tougher et al. 2012). Via AMFm, the Global Fund subsidized not only governments but also Big Pharma and private purchasers in LICs (Oxfam 2012).

Perhaps most importantly, and relevant to our topic, none of the SIHI case studies, including those examined in this section, perform well against UHC's (limited) standards of universalism, service comprehensiveness, and financial protection. CCPF provides health information but does not help meet the urgent need for obstetric care in rural Malawi. The private drug sellers recruited to the Ugandan project delivered only three treatments for fever, with no attention to health promotion and prevention (a critique that may be extended to the iCCM strategy more broadly), and failed to strengthen primary care in rural Uganda. The primary care package on offer at OFHR posts in rural Rwanda is limited, and the government subsidizes CBHI premiums only for a section of the poor (identified through a fraught process), which means that those who are not covered have to either pay fully or forego OFHR services. None of the project evaluations reported on the perverse incentives that may be created when provider income is directly linked to service use. As the social innovations themselves tend to rely on unpaid/poorly paid community workers, usually women, such narrow approaches to primary care reinforce gender-based inequality and exploitation. In the next section, we explore alternatives to the social innovation zeitgeist that suggest that other avenues exist.

4 Towards Healthcare Justice in the Majority World

Corporate involvement in healthcare is widely hailed and backed by multilaterals, philanthropies, and private sector donors, who themselves pose as the prime option for shoring up healthcare systems. Less deliberated are the role of government and the publicly funded and implemented primary care models that have a proven track record in various Majority World settings. This section delves into three such PHC 'success stories' – from Sri Lanka, Thailand, and Cuba – to illuminate the ways in which they differ from the mixed public–private model of UHC guiding the piecemeal primary care 'innovations' described in Section 3. Each PHC system discussed here is internationally recognized for providing accessible, comprehensive healthcare (Kruk et al. 2010).

We first explore the delivery of maternal and infant care in Sri Lanka to showcase how a non-fee-levying community-based service that relies on a strong network of primary healthcare facilities and grassroots health workers further universal access and equity. Sri Lanka's approach contrasts markedly from the mhealth solutions for maternal and child health championed by dominant global health players. Second, we outline the policies and measures guiding Thailand's retention of health workers in rural areas, patently different from more typical piecemeal approaches to training community workers who must then generate their own income, or pay hefty franchise royalties, in the name of 'sustainability'. Finally, we review PHC implementation in Cuba, focusing on the Family Doctor and Nurse Programme, to illustrate how truly universal and comprehensive PHC is possible when adequate public resources are directed towards it.

Each case study begins with a description of the setting and the PHC initiative, and then places it in historical context and within the broader healthcare system. Here, we showcase how each programme was shaped by context-specific social and political forces and actors, rather than through a set of technocratic or entrepreneurial interventions. We conclude by observing that the success of all three experiences is undergirded by overwhelmingly public financing, administration, and delivery of healthcare, often in the face of Global Health Inc.

Universal and 'Free' Maternal and Infant Care in Sri Lanka

Sri Lanka, a South Asian island-nation of about 22 million people, has had long-standing debt problems that have reached crisis proportions in recent years, leading the country to default on its debt repayments in 2022. With a 2021 GDP per capita of (current) USD 4014 (World Bank 2023), the World Bank downgraded Sri Lanka in 2020 from its short-lived 'upper-middle-income' status to a 'lower-middle-income' country (Daily FT 2020). Still, women's literacy remains relatively high at 92 per cent and the country reports health indicators on par with upper middle-income countries. Over 80 per cent of the population resides in rural areas (World Bank 2023), where the non-fee-levying public healthcare system plays a key role in service delivery. Notwithstanding periods of both economic crisis and civil war since the 1970s, in 1985, Sri Lanka was featured among a handful of health equity exemplars in the Rockefeller Foundation's *Good Health at Low Cost* study (Halstead et al. 1985).

Decades on, Sri Lanka's public system of maternal and infant care receives international praise, even as such acclaim often obscures the centrality of its public dimensions (Levine and Kinder 2004). Today, the country maintains near-universal coverage of prenatal care (99 per cent) and skilled attendance at birth (99 per cent). An overwhelming majority (95 per cent) of deliveries take place at public facilities; over 90 per cent of postpartum women receive a home visit from their midwife within the first ten days, with roughly eight home visits per infant (Department of Census and Statistics 2017; Family Health Bureau 2021).

The maternal mortality ratio (MMR) at 36 deaths per 100,000 live births in 2017, was twice the OECD average and roughly equal to Thailand and Cuba's MMR, but far lower than LMIC (231 deaths per 100,000 live births) and MIC (184 deaths per 100,000 live births) averages, and lower than the upper middle-income average of 41 deaths per 100,000 live births (World Bank 2023). Neonatal and infant mortality rates at 4 and 6 per 1,000 live births, respectively in 2017, were lower than the upper-middle income averages of 6 and 9 deaths per 1,000 live births (World Bank 2023). With more than 80 per cent of infants exclusively breastfed in their first six months (Family Health Bureau 2021), Sri Lanka reports one of the highest breastfeeding rates in the world (World Breast Feeding Trends Initiative (WBTI) 2023). The non-fee-levying public healthcare system is often credited for the country's maternal and infant health achievements, although decades of welfare investment in education, water, sanitation, and food subsidies/supplementation are an important part of this success story (Haththotuwa et al. 2012; Pathmanathan et al. 2003).

A Truly *Public Maternal and Infant Care Service*

Maternal and infant care is an integral part of the Ministry of Health's Family Health Programme, guided by the National Policy on Maternal and Child Health (2012) that aims to achieve the 'highest possible levels of health' among 'all women, children and families through provision of comprehensive, sustainable, equitable and quality maternal and child health services' (Ministry of Health Sri Lanka 2012). The Family Health Programme encompasses pre-conception, antenatal, intrapartum, postpartum, newborn, infant, and child care, school and adolescent health services, family planning, nutritional support, and oral health services, with gender-based violence prevention a recent addition (Family Health Bureau 2021).

The preventive and curative arms of the public healthcare system are administered separately and offer distinct services linked by referral systems. Preventive maternal and infant care is decentralized to the provinces and delivered via about 350 medical officer of health (MOH) areas – roughly corresponding to government administrative divisions – each serving approximately 50,000 people. A public health team comprising doctors, nurses, midwives, and others, delivers maternal, infant, and other services within each MOH area. Curative services are purveyed through tiered healthcare facilities at primary, secondary, and tertiary levels across the country, including two specialized hospitals each for women and children (Kumar 2019). In 2015, there were 517 and 77 hospitals, offering basic and comprehensive emergency obstetric (and neonatal) care, respectively (WHO 2016b).

Public health midwives are the backbone of the system, providing grassroots services that encompass home- and clinic-based care within public health midwife areas (one midwife per 3,000–5,000 people). A referral system connects community-based maternal and infant care to hospital-based specialist services. Public health midwives make a remarkable contribution to health promotion by carrying out local health education campaigns, especially focused on maternal and child nutrition. Intimately connected with their communities, they also play an advocacy role at the village level on health and social matters (Daniel 2016; Kumar 2019).

Albeit resource-constrained, this system functions in every district with no charges at points of delivery. Once registered in the system, women and children are followed up at home, at community polyclinics, and at specialist units of local hospitals under a system of 'shared care'. Maternal and feto-infant mortality surveillance and response systems track and review each maternal and perinatal death, enhancing quality and accountability (Family Health Bureau 2021).

Origins and Expansion of Free Maternal and Infant Care

The antecedents of Sri Lanka's public maternal and infant care system are traced back to nineteenth-century 'British Ceylon', when some of Britain's emerging public health policies began to be transferred to its 'model colony' driven by imperial exigencies (Jones 2002). Though institutionalized forms of indigenous maternity care predated colonization by several centuries (Pathmanathan et al. 2003), it was in 1897, under British colonial rule, that the first 'lying-in home' was established for delivering mothers, in Colombo. Midwifery training began in 1906, with mandatory registration as of the 1920s (Jones 2002).

The MOH system that is central to present-day community-based maternal and infant care, meanwhile, has its roots in the system of local health units introduced by the Rockefeller Foundation in the early twentieth-century. Arriving in 1915 to assist the colonial government with a hookworm disease scourge on tea plantations, the Foundation oversaw a 1916–1922 campaign to treat plantation workers with anthelminthic medicines to attenuate hookworm-induced anaemia. Stymied by the Planters' Association, who were unwilling to invest in sanitation, the campaign was mostly fruitless, compelling the Foundation to shift its public health work to the suburbs of Colombo, where it established Ceylon's first health unit in 1926. Within three years, five health units were established, serving about 5 per cent of the population. A dearth of midwives spurred a special midwifery training programme that was confined to Colombo and a few other townships until the 1930s (Hewa 1995, 2011; Jones 2002).

Expansion of healthcare to rural areas took place in conjunction with the granting of universal franchise (1931), part of Ceylon's transition to self-governance. Thereafter, elected State Councillors were compelled to address the demands of their electorates, amid a strengthening left movement and economic depression. The 1934/35 malaria epidemic saw a rapid expansion of health units, and a doubling (within three years) of trained midwives to work at health units in rural areas and on plantations (Jones 2002; Pathmanathan et al. 2003; Silva 2014). In parallel, the health units oversaw large-scale water and sanitation projects (Hewa 2011).

The dominance of Marxist parties and trade unions in Ceylon's anti-colonial movement pushed the government to prioritize social welfare. The Suriya-Mal Movement, launched in the early 1930s to protest the sale of poppies on Remembrance Day, was active in malaria relief work, and organized collectively to demand state investment in rural healthcare (Silva 2014). Food subsidies came into effect in the early 1940s, together with a food-rationing scheme to address food scarcity during World War II. 'Free education', originating in the Swabasha (vernacular language) Movement, became government policy in 1945, with universal primary and secondary (and later tertiary) education becoming citizen rights (Wickramasinghe 2006).

The 'Free Health' policy (1951), which eliminated user charges from previously fee-levying units at public hospitals, came on the heels of independence in 1948 (Perera 1985; Wickramasinghe 2006), and has guided the financing, administration, and delivery of healthcare services ever since. Public sector maternal and infant care has remained 'free' throughout the country's post-independence history, although fast eroding under economic crisis.

Current Provenance of Overall Healthcare System Resources

Under the Free Health policy, the tax-funded public healthcare system remains the dominant provider in the country. With about 4 per cent of GDP invested in healthcare, the state contributes just under 50 per cent of health spending, equivalent to a per capita government health expenditure of (current) USD 76 – about 9 per cent of the government budget in 2019 (World Bank 2023). The public system purveys approximately 90 per cent of inpatient admissions, 50 per cent of outpatient visits, and the bulk of preventive care (Smith 2018).

Although the proportion of health expenditure devoted to public health programmes has declined over the years, and is currently at about 5 per cent (Institute for Health Policy 2021), maternal and child health receives the largest share from this allocation (Ministry of Health Sri Lanka 2018). The majority of pregnant and childbearing women access the public sector for inpatient and delivery care (Department of Census and Statistics 2017), but increasingly rely on a combination of public and private services for prenatal care (Kumar 2020). Reliance on the public sector is similarly high for newborn and infant care (Family Health Bureau 2021).

Most categories of health workers serving in the public system are trained on a non-fee-levying basis under the country's deep-rooted Free Education policy. Public health midwives complete a fully subsidized eighteen-month midwifery diploma programme, comprising one year at school and six months in field training. Public health nurses possess a three-year nursing diploma plus additional midwifery and field training. The diploma-granting schools are located country-wide, facilitating training in 'home' districts; students also receive a stipend to cover day-to-day expenses (Pathmanathan et al. 2003; Senanayake et al. 2011). Medical officers of health – general doctors with public health training – mostly graduate from non-fee-levying state medical schools, which together train about 80 per cent of medical graduates, annually (De Silva 2017). Health workers in the curative arm of the public system also mostly train within this system, and the Ministry of Health subsidizes postgraduate training of its specialist cadre, including the obstetricians who serve at public sector referral units at secondary and tertiary care centres.

Newly graduated health workers are required to serve at assigned postings for a minimum period (usually 2–4 years), ensuring a widely dispersed health workforce (Kumar 2019). Because the public sector is still the dominant healthcare provider and guarantees full-time salaried employment for most health professionals, the Ministry of Health has been able to retain staff, although brain drain has markedly increased since the onset of the economic crisis.

Challenges Ahead

Despite historical commitments to Free Health, decades of underinvestment in the public system and targeted incentives to the private sector have amplified the latter's role in healthcare. This trajectory of health reform has affected the public sector maternal and infant care service, with many households accessing fee-levying private outpatient care, facilitated by dual practice (Kumar et al. 2022). The more recent expansion of employer-based health insurance has partly contributed to a rising proportion of private sector deliveries taking place at hotel-like commercial hospitals, which offer tiered packages of luxury services (see Hemas Hospitals 2022). This mixed public–private system has resulted in increasing levels of out-of-pocket expenditures and stratified service delivery (Kumar 2019).

Existing urban-rural inequities are intensified by maldistribution as well as brain drain, affecting rural districts. In 2017, 620 specialists, 4,745 medical officers and 8,562 nurses served in the Colombo District, compared with 147 specialists, 1,208 medical officers and 1,234 nurses in all five districts of the war-torn Northern Province (Ministry of Health Sri Lanka 2019). Few career advancement opportunities exist for non-physician public health personnel (including midwives), making the sector less appealing for employment. Even as the government has no specific policies in place to recruit or retain health workers in rural areas, the rapid exodus of health professionals in the context of the ongoing economic crisis is crippling the system (Kumar 2022). Atop the brain drain, a lack of foreign currency reserves has induced widespread shortages in essential medicines and supplies across the public sector (Vaidyanathan 2023).

In sum, Sri Lanka's maternal and infant care service is a product of the country's publicly financed and delivered 'free' healthcare system. Rather than a set of technocratic interventions, this system has evolved – shaped by multiple political and economic factors, including claims on the state made during economic depression and independence struggles – and persisted across distinct regimes, with strong popular support. The country's achievements in maternal and infant care rely heavily on public health infrastructure and a public sector-trained healthcare workforce, including and especially a cadre of public health midwives, delivering infant and maternal care at the grassroots level. Still, privatization, a health worker brain drain, and the ongoing economic crisis, threaten Sri Lanka's Free Health policy and the PHC system.

Thailand's Efforts to Build a Rural Healthcare Workforce

Thailand is an 'upper-middle income country' that just fifty years ago was classified as 'low-income' by the World Bank (n.d.b). At (current) USD 7,066 in 2021, the GDP per capita in Thailand is double that of Sri Lanka (World Bank 2023). With a life expectancy at birth of seventy-nine years, Thailand is well known for its UHC achievements, built on strengthening health infrastructure, expanding the health workforce, and extending financial risk protection (Tangcharoensathien et al. 2018). About half (48 per cent in 2021) of Thailand's population of 71 million lives in rural areas (World Bank 2023), most of whom rely on district health systems – the primary provider in rural localities (Tangcharoensathien et al. 2018).

Each district health system comprises ten to twelve health centres and a district hospital serving about 50,000 people. Rural health centres typically serve 3,000–5,000 people each, and offer health promotion, disease prevention, basic curative care, and (more recently) rehabilitation and long-term care, delivered by a team of 3–4 non-physician health workers. District hospitals support outpatient service delivery, directly and via the health centres, while also offering inpatient services. On average, district hospital staff include 3–4 general practitioners, 30 nurses, 2–3 pharmacists, 1–2 dentists, 20 paramedics, plus support workers; some also have specialist cadres. The regional and provincial hospitals, which function as referral centres, deliver secondary and tertiary care, while at the grassroots, trained village health volunteers (VHV; one per ten to twenty households) receive a small honorarium to carry out health promotion, deliver contraceptives and provide other basic care (Pagaiya et al. 2021; Pongpirul 2020; Tangcharoensathien et al. 2018; WHO 2017).

A Programme to Retain Rural Health Workers

Thailand reports 0.9 physicians and 3.2 nurses per 1000 population (World Bank 2023), a little under the WHO composite standard of 4.5 doctors, nurses, and midwives per 1,000 population (WHO 2016a). The strength of Thailand's health workforce is its nurses (on par with the upper-middle income country average of 3.3 nurses per 1,000 population) and village health volunteers (upwards of one million) (WHO 2015, 2017; World Bank 2023). Created via deliberate policymaking, Thailand's rural health workforce is sustained by long-standing rural retention strategies (Pagaiya and Noree 2009; Tangcharoensathien et al. 2018).

To counter the increasing migration of doctors to the West in the 1960s, Thailand implemented a government bond for newly graduated medical professionals that mandated three years of service in a rural locality. Similar bonds ensued for other health professionals, including nurses, dentists, and pharmacists. For some four decades, all graduating health professionals had to complete mandatory rural placements, with sizeable penalties for those who did not comply. Because training programmes were (and still are) heavily subsidized by the government, mandating rural service did not encounter public opposition (Patcharanarumol et al. 2011), and health worker resistance was attenuated by guarantees of full-time work in the public system. However, even as rural retention remained a challenge, a 2002 public sector downsizing policy, implemented as part of a World Bank-supported reform project, ended guaranteed public sector employment for some categories of health workers. Today, apart from doctors and dentists, most health professionals (including nurses) are not assured of state employment and cannot be mandated to complete rural placements (Pagaiya and Noree 2009; WHO 2015).

A second strategy, since the 1990s, has been to recruit candidates from rural areas into health professional programmes, with requirements to serve in the 'home' locality for a stipulated period (Pagaiya and Noree 2009). The Collaborative Project to Increase Production of Rural Doctors (CPIPRD, est. 1994) and the One District One Doctor (ODOD, est. 2005) programme, both operating between the ministries of education and public health, enable rural students who score somewhat lower marks on highly competitive national entrance examinations to enrol in medical programmes with a quid pro quo of service. CPIPRD, for students from mixed urban-rural districts, requires graduates to serve for three years in Ministry of Public Health hospitals. The ODOD programme targets students from remote areas with full scholarships, then twelve-year mandatory service in 'home' districts. Doctors who graduate from these programmes – about 30–40 per cent of the country's annual output – are more likely to remain in public service even beyond their mandated period (Arora et al. 2017; Nithiapinyasakul et al. 2016; Pagaiya et al. 2015; Tangcharoensathien et al. 2018). Similarly, colleges of nursing and public health recruit locally with full government-funded scholarships. Atop their state-subsidized education, students receive support for basic necessities like clothing, accommodation, food, and learning materials (Pagaiya and Noree 2009; Tangcharoensathien et al. 2018; Wibulpolprasert and Pengpaibon 2003).

Third, health professional curricula, including in medicine, are rurally oriented and conducted in the Thai language. Curricula place emphasis on primary care and public health, with practical training in rural settings (Pagaiya and Noree 2009; Wibulpolprasert and Pengpaibon 2003). Rurally focused curricula serve to dissuade international physician migration and also reduce the urban elite bias in access to medical education. Fourth, the government incentivizes rural work through the provision of hardship allowances and overtime payments, alongside specific mechanisms recognizing rural service, including awards and opportunities for career advancement (Tangcharoensathien et al. 2018; Wibulpolprasert and Fleck 2014). In 2008, physicians serving in rural districts received 10–15 per cent more in monthly salaries than counterparts in urban public facilities; these allowances have increased over time (Pagaiya et al. 2012).

The multi-professional Thai rural health workforce is complemented by rural health volunteers, also recruited locally. The VHV programme, initiated in 1977 in concert with WHO's Health for All strategy, engages the services of grass-roots community health workers in health promotion, prevention, and more recently, long-term care (Pagaiya et al. 2021; Pongpirul 2020). VHV are well-respected community members; they are nominated by residents, must be ≥18 years, resident in the area for ≥6 months, literate, and have a history of employment. Once selected, they must follow classroom training and pass an examination. VHV provide services to a designated group of households, supervised by local primary care workers. At the programme's inception, the health volunteers worked without payment but now receive a small monthly stipend from the Ministry of Public Health (Pongpirul 2020; Treerutkuarkul 2008).

Decades-Long Public Investment in Healthcare

Thailand stands out as a Majority World country that has never been colonised, although various colonial missions were active in Siam (later Thailand) following treaties between the Thai monarchy and colonial powers. As such, Western medicine made inroads into the well-established system of Thai Indigenous medicine in the nineteenth-century, catering primarily to elites and the monarchy (Charuluxananan and Chentanez 2007; Gosling 1985). Early investment in public health is credited to Prince Mahidol Adulyadej (1892–1929), celebrated in Thailand for his influential role, especially in health professions education, paving the way for multi-professional health workforce development programmes (Muangman 1987).

The shift from an absolute to a constitutional monarchy in 1932 saw successive governments gradually expand health services to rural areas, albeit thwarted by frequent coups that placed the country under repressive military regimes (Patcharanarumol et al. 2011). The country's first National Economic and Social Development Plan, formulated in 1961 under a military regime, launched an extensive programme of economic development (Ayal 1962). Then, from the 1970s to 1990s, rural development accelerated, at times to counter the perceived threat of communism, with heavy investment in rural infrastructure for health, education, and agriculture (Tangcharoensathien et al. 2018).

Student uprisings in 1973 set the stage for democratic elections in 1975. The newly elected government implemented a medical welfare scheme that covered the country's poor in line with the Third National Economic and Social Development Plan. Emerging during this period of student activism, a group of young medical doctors formed the Rural Doctors' Movement. Later renamed the Rural Doctors' Society in the face of state clampdown on communist organizing, the Movement addressed rural health concerns while functioning as a mutual support group for doctors working in under-resourced district health systems (Harris 2017; Wibulpolprasert and Fleck 2014). Paradoxically, political instability created more space for techno-bureaucrats to intervene in policy matters. Rural Doctors' Society members, who would later hold key positions with the Ministry of Public Health, played a critical role in implementing the 2002 universal coverage scheme (UCS) (Harris 2017; Tangcharoensathien et al. 2018).

Thailand began its PHC programme as part of its Fourth National Economic and Social Development Plan in 1977, as the Alma-Ata conference plans were unfolding. Having identified the lack of community participation as an impediment to rural health, the government introduced the VHV programme, first piloted in a number of villages, and then scaled up to cover the entire country (Pongpirul 2020). The government made vast investments in rural health infrastructure in the 1980s, temporarily halting the build-up of urban hospitals to channel funds to the district health systems. By the 1990s, each district had a hospital, each subdistrict a health centre, and almost every village a rural health post (Tangcharoensathien et al. 2018; Tungsubutra 1976). Parallel investments were made in health professional education, resulting in soaring numbers of graduating doctors, nurses, dentists, and pharmacists; between 1990 and 2009, the number of doctors in Thailand doubled from 12,000 to 24,000, while the ranks of professional nurses rose from about 40,000 to 110,000 (WHO 2015).

Most notable in recent times is Thailand's commitment to UHC through its 2002 UCS, which derived from an election promise and was implemented against the advice of WHO and World Bank experts, given the dire state of Thailand's economy at the time. Importantly, UCS garnered the full backing of government bureaucrats and Ministry of Public Health officials, a number of them hailing from the Rural Doctors' Society (Harris 2017; Wibulpolprasert and Fleck 2014).

Current Provenance of Overall Healthcare System Resources

In 2019, Thailand spent 3.8 per cent of its GDP and 13.9 per cent of the government budget on health (World Bank 2023). Health financing is sourced through general taxes, social insurance contributions, private insurance premiums, and direct out-of-pocket payments (WHO 2017). Almost three-quarters of health spending comes from public sources, amounting to per capita (current) USD 212 government spending on health in 2019. Out-of-pocket spending is low at less than 10 per cent, and a negligible share of health expenditures is financed by external sources (World Bank 2023).

UCS covers healthcare for over 70 per cent of the population and dominates in rural areas. The remaining population is covered by the Civil Servants Medical Benefits Scheme (CSMB, 7 per cent) – for government employees, their dependents, and pensioners – and Social Health Insurance (SHI, 20 per cent), catering to private formal sector workers. UCS and CSMB are financed through general taxes, while SHI is a social security arrangement with tripartite contributions from employees, employers, and the government. All three schemes are administered by public agencies (WHO 2015, 2017).

Theoretically underpinned by a 'purchaser-provider split', where purchasing takes place through the National Health Security Office (NHSO) and provision through public and private providers, in reality, Thailand has retained state purview over both purchasing and provision. NHSO is an independent state agency, and 95 per cent of UCS-covered services are publicly provided in rural areas through the district health systems. The UCS and NHSO were created by the National Health Security Act (2002), under which every individual is registered with the nearest primary health centre and entitled to receive comprehensive healthcare services from that centre or via facilitated referrals to higher centres. The NHSO is empowered to demand adequate financial allocation for its purchasing system from the finance ministry (Sundararaman 2018). Accountability is built into the system through the National Health Act (2007), which created the National Health Commission, tasked with organizing annual public hearings or national health assemblies with beneficiaries and service providers (Kantamaturapoj et al. 2020).

Although the health insurance schemes operating in Thailand offer varying degrees of coverage and UCS excludes undocumented migrant workers, by and large they cover a comprehensive set of services. UCS offers health promotion and preventive services for all, including citizens covered by other schemes. It also covers comprehensive primary through tertiary care, recently extended to renal replacement therapy on the grounds of equity as this treatment was previously covered only by the other two schemes (Tangcharoensathien et al. 2018; WHO 2015).

Often neglected in accounts of the Thai health system is the overwhelming role played by the public sector in healthcare delivery (Tangcharoensathien et al. 2018). In 2015, public providers comprised 9,768 health centres, 734 district hospitals, 97 provincial and regional hospitals and 48 specialized hospitals under the Ministry of Public Health, and 365 medical centres and 60 hospitals under other ministries (WHO 2017). Although large in number, Thailand's 17,000 plus private clinics and 11,000 plus private pharmacies are primarily concentrated in Bangkok, as are private hospitals – totalling over 300 (WHO 2019). Private clinics are mostly run by solo practitioners who also work in the public system (Prakongsai 2005). Private hospitals are small in scale, except the fifty-plus hospitals catering to medical tourists (Noree et al. 2016). In 2015, the private sector accounted for only 14 per cent of outpatient visits and 11 per cent of inpatient admissions (Tangcharoensathien et al. 2018).

Thailand offers multiple lessons of potential interest for Majority World (and Minority World) governments. Retaining purchasing has enabled the Thai government to control costs through monopsonistic bargaining and confining prescription to generics in a National Essential Medicines List (Tangcharoensathien et al. 2018; WHO 2015). It has skilfully invoked the World Trade Organization's Trade Related Aspects of Intellectual Property Rights (TRIPS) agreement to issue compulsory licenses for medicines and devices for non-commercial public sector use (Wibulpolprasert and Fleck 2014). Thailand's achievements are bolstered by several autonomous public sector organizations, including the Health Systems Research Institute (1992) and the Thai Health Promotion Foundation (2001), the latter financed through excise taxes (WHO 2015).

Challenges Ahead

Brain drain from public to private sector remains a nagging problem in the Thai health system. Doctors, nurses, and other health professionals increasingly opt to work at private facilities in urban localities despite the government's ongoing rural retention initiatives. While deliberate downsizing of the public sector since 2002 has contributed to the problem (WHO 2015), a major driver of brain drain today is medical tourism, promoted by the Thai government since 2003 to boost the economy. Lucrative remuneration packages, much higher than public sector salaries, entice public sector health workers to relocate to urban areas to serve in hotel-like commercial hospitals for medical tourists and Thai elites (Harris and Maia 2022; Noree et al. 2016).

Internal brain drain has tended to accelerate during periods of private health sector growth, first, during Thailand's late 1980s/early 1990s economic boom, and then in the 2000s during recovery from the 1997 economic crisis. In the interim period, health workers remained in the public sector, as job opportunities in the private sector dwindled (Pagaiya and Noree 2009; WHO 2015), reflecting the private sector's impact on equity of access. Importantly, brain drain has intensified urban-rural inequities (Harris and Maia 2022) with a sizeable proportion of services delivered by urban commercial hospitals consumed by Thai elites (Noree et al. 2016).

In sum, Thailand has taken a series of policy measures to retain health workers in rural areas. These measures, complemented by investments in public health infrastructure, public sector-driven health professional programmes, and

UCS, have enabled Thailand to advance UHC. However, several structural challenges remain, namely internal migration of health workers and state-backed privatization initiatives, including medical tourism, that are undermining rural retention, and segmenting healthcare between rich and poor.

Comprehensive Community-Oriented PHC in Cuba

Cuba is classified as an 'upper-middle income country' with a population of about 11 million and a GDP per capita of (current) USD 9,500 (World Bank 2023). A trailblazer in PHC (initiated before Alma-Ata), Cuba has been largely overlooked by the mainstream, arguably for political reasons since it has been under Communist Party governance since shortly after the 1959 revolution (Cooper et al. 2006). With free education, spanning primary through tertiary levels, the country reports a female literacy rate of 100 per cent. Cuba's health indicators are superior to those of Sri Lanka and Thailand, with mortality rates among neonates, infants, and young children even below OECD averages. Among many milestones, Cuba was declared malaria-free by WHO in 1973, was early to eliminate measles (1993), and, in 2015, became the first country to eliminate mother-to-child transmission of HIV and syphilis (Lenzer 2016; Pineo 2019).

Cuba's healthcare system is centrally planned, with financing, administration, and delivery under the state's purview for over six decades. Citizens access services on a non-fee-levying basis under the country's universal health policy. Healthcare is delivered via tiered institutions; at the grassroots level, 10,000 plus teams of family doctors and nurses offer clinic and home-based care, linked to local polyclinics. Roughly 500 polyclinics form the backbone of Cuba's PHC system and are connected to some 150 secondary and tertiary level referral centres (Pineo 2019; Serrate 2019).

Each polyclinic serves approximately 30,000 people, offering a range of primary and secondary level outpatient services, including accident and emergency care, reproductive, maternal and child health services, chronic disease care, and care for seniors. The polyclinics are staffed by multi-professional teams, including family physicians and medical specialists, other health professionals (psychologists, physiotherapists, etc.) and social workers. They are equipped to provide comprehensive diagnostic services, and also certain advanced procedures, with the subset of services tailored to the needs of the local community (Keck and Reed 2012; Pineo 2019).

The Family Doctor and Nurse Programme

The Family Doctor and Nurse Programme (FDNP), incorporated into the PHC system in the 1980s, originally placed one family doctor and nurse team in each neighbourhood of about 120–150 families or 600–800 residents. Since 2011, when Cuba adopted a series of market-oriented reforms, the population served by a family doctor-nurse team has risen, reaching roughly 1,500 residents in urban areas, while remaining closer to the original number in rural localities. Teams are also posted to schools, senior homes and work settings, and now include public health personnel (Cárdenas et al. 2018; Keck and Reed 2012; Pineo 2019).

Family doctor and nurse teams operate from consultorios – clinics located within each neighbourhood. Having residential facilities within the consultorio facilitates greater involvement of the health team in the local community (Cárdenas et al. 2018; Keck and Reed 2012). Clinics are conducted in the mornings, and home visits in the afternoons. Each resident is visited at home at least twice a year with more frequent visits undertaken when needed. For instance, newborns are seen fortnightly in the first six months, and monthly thereafter through twelve months (Rodriguez et al. 2008). Uniquely, FDNP integrates health promotion, disease prevention, and treatment, with services delivered on a continuum of care, alongside action on other vital PHC components (water, sanitation, environment, etc.; Birn et al. 2017; Pineo 2019). In addition, FDNP teams play a central role in health promotion campaigns, with keen community involvement (Keck and Reed 2012; Swanson et al. 1995).

FDNP is designed to ensure ongoing assessment and health status evaluation at household and population levels. Detailed health records are maintained for each household documenting vulnerability to disease based on Ministry of Public Health protocols. Tailored interventions are delivered at the household level, with trends monitored to assess progress. Data are then compiled and conveyed to polyclinics and to the national level (Cárdenas et al. 2018; Keck and Reed 2012). While such monitoring is sometimes construed as intrusive, it has enabled the Cuban authorities to achieve noteworthy results (Pineo 2019).

Building PHC After a Revolution

Prior to Cuba's 1959 revolution, healthcare facilities and practitioners were concentrated in the capital, Havana, where the private sector was the main service provider. Healthcare delivery was fragmented, unregulated, and focused on curative care, with virtually no attention to health promotion or disease prevention. After the revolution, as thousands of doctors fled to Miami, the Rural Medical Service was established in 1960, to bring healthcare to rural and remote areas. Authorities initially focused on controlling infections and reducing maternal mortality, alongside parallel investments in water, sanitation, and agricultural systems, plus other redistributive measures. In the 1970s, the Cuban government gradually brought all healthcare and other health-related institutions, including private facilities, under the Ministry of Public Health (Fernandez 1975; Navarro 1972).

As a result of the medical exodus, the government established medical schools, previously confined to Havana, in rural areas to facilitate rural recruitment and retention of physicians. Community-oriented medical curricula emphasized public health and community service over curative care and material gain (Keck and Reed 2012; Navarro 1972). These were accompanied by schools to train nurses, technicians, auxiliaries, and other health professionals, to ensure adequate health worker cadres. In the 1970s, after the extension of public hospitals to rural areas, the government decentralised PHC to areas (approx. 30,000 population) and sectors (approx. 3,000 population). Each area hosted a polyclinic delivering clinical, environmental health, public health, and social services. All graduating physicians were appointed to hospitals and polyclinics, fulfilling 2-year mandatory rural postings (Fernandez 1975; Navarro 1972).

The Communist-led government channelled resources to crucial areas outside the health sector, including education, housing, nutrition, and employment, with more than 50 per cent of the government budget devoted to education and health by the early 1960s. From the outset, Cuba's PHC system involved a high degree of community participation and mass mobilization. The People's Commissions on Health, established under the Popular Councils, comprising mostly women, included representation from mass organizations such as the Committee for the Defense of the Revolution, Federation of Cuban Women, farmers' organizations, and trade unions (Fernandez 1975; Navarro 1972).

The effects of the US embargo, imposed on Cuba just two years after the revolution, were minimized thanks to assistance from the Soviet Union as well as vibrant trade with the socialist bloc. After the dissolution of the Soviet Union in the early 1990s and the US's ratcheting up of embargo conditions, the economic situation deteriorated, with far-reaching consequences. US penalties imposed on ships that docked in Cuba resulted in shortages of essential imports, including food items, medical equipment, and pharmaceuticals. Malnutrition in certain populations (not pregnant women or children, who continued to be prioritized), plus shortages of chlorine and soap, saw rising rates of infectious diseases (Garfield and Santana 1997; Pineo 2019). Fuel and fertilizer/pesticide shortages led to increased reliance on bicycle transport and urban organic farming, both with salutary effects (Birn et al. 2017). An unexpected outcome of the US embargo, Cuba's cutting-edge biotechnology and pharmaceutical sectors have paid off over the years: Cuba is a lead manufacturer of vaccines and biologics, including Covid-19 vaccines, which are being distributed worldwide free of patents (Pineo 2019; Taylor 2022).

Current Provenance of Overall Healthcare System Resources

In 2019, Cuba spent 11.3 per cent of its GDP on the health sector, accounting for about 16 per cent of general government expenditures, and translating to a per capita government expenditure of (current) USD 921 (World Bank 2023), four times Thailand's and over ten times Sri Lanka's government health spending. Government expenditure accounts for 89 per cent of total health spending, with private (out-of-pocket) expenditure comparatively low at 11 per cent in 2019. The involvement of external actors/donors is minimal, accounting for <1 per cent of total health spending, as in Sri Lanka and Thailand. Cuba's health infrastructure is financed, administered, and delivered by the government with no separation of purchasing and provision. Out-of-pocket expenditures are mostly driven by cost-sharing on medicines and unaddressed senior care needs, such as prosthetics, hearing aids, and wheelchairs. The health workforce is trained at state schools on a non-fee-levying basis (Gonzalez et al. 2018; Pineo 2019; Serrate 2019).

Cuban health statistics speak for themselves. Life expectancy at birth is seventy-eight years and neonatal and infant mortality are on par with 'developed' nations at 2 and 4 deaths per 1,000 live births, respectively, in 2017. Maternal mortality at 36 deaths per 100,000 live births is similar to that of Sri Lanka and Thailand. Cuba boasts high numbers of healthcare providers per capita, even by HIC standards; 7.6 nurses/midwives and 8.4 physicians per 1,000 population, the latter being the highest in the world (World Bank 2023). However, these figures are somewhat inflated because they include the sizeable proportion (up to one-quarter) of the health workforce that serves internationally in Cuba's medical missions (Pineo 2019).

Cuba's health diplomacy strategy has, since the 1960s, required a high output of health professionals. Originally a solidarity effort (with no quid pro quo) to reciprocate support to countries that had helped Cuba's revolution effort or that were engaged in similar struggles, today Cuba's international medical cooperation programme is its largest source of foreign income. Cuban medical teams currently work in many Majority World settings, even serving in several European countries at the height of the Covid-19 pandemic. Between 2011 and 2016, over 140,000[6] health professionals from Cuba served in sixty-seven countries; in twenty countries, Cuba covered all associated expenses (De Vos 2019). At any given time, Cuba has about 50,000 trainees at domestic medical schools and counterparts established elsewhere, mostly on a non-fee-levying basis, on the condition that graduated doctors return to serve in their home

---

[6] This number reflects the total number of health professionals sent abroad as members of Cuba's medical missions during the specified period, not the total number of health professionals working abroad at any given time.

localities. This includes tens of thousands of health professionals trained through the Latin American Medical School (ELAM) in Havana, thus supporting dozens of countries to address brain drain and health worker shortages (Kirk 2015; Pineo 2019).

Challenges Ahead

Since 2011, when Cuba adopted market-oriented economic reforms, policymakers are striving to improve the 'efficiency' of Cuba's PHC system through modernization and cost-cutting measures, such as rationing, reorganizing, regionalizing, and downsizing healthcare services. These reforms have resulted in cuts to administrative and management cadres in the health sector, upward revision of the target population for FDNP teams, and accelerating the country's international medical cooperation, now a major source of income (Gonzalez et al. 2018; Ojeda et al. 2018).

The large numbers of Cuban doctors serving in medical missions abroad have prompted criticism regarding domestic physician shortages in some areas, manifesting in delays to care (Brotherton 2013). Salaries remain low and stagnant, prompting some health workers, including medical professionals, to pursue non-health work, for instance, in the tourism industry. A small proportion of doctors (approx. 3 per cent) who participate in foreign missions abandon their work to relocate to greener pastures, facilitated until 2017 by the US government's Cuban Medical Professional Parole Program (Campion and Morrisey 2013; Pineo 2019).

The ongoing impact of the US embargo presents a huge challenge to the sustainability of Cuba's PHC system. Despite government commitment to universal, comprehensive PHC, a growing proportion of health expenditure is financed by households. A large oil-for-doctors exchange with Venezuela's Chávez administration starting in the early 2000s was helpful but the escalating economic crisis in Venezuela and the impact of the pandemic on tourism have worsened Cuba's economic situation (Becker 2021). As the blockade continues, Cuba is having trouble acquiring essential medical equipment and materials (Ojeda et al. 2018; Pineo 2019).

In sum, Cuba's state-financed, administered, and delivered PHC system has achieved remarkable results. The FDNP brings healthcare services closer to the people, integrating primary care services with health promotion and action on the social determinants of health. Throughout its post-revolutionary history, Cuba has prioritised investments in health, even in the face of economic crisis; the US-imposed embargo stimulated nimble developments in biotechnology and health diplomacy, both key sources of foreign exchange. In the face of adverse economic conditions, however, the country's health sector is vulnerable to deeper funding cuts, with potentially dire consequences for public health.

Contrasting Approaches

This analysis of PHC initiatives in Sri Lanka, Thailand, and Cuba points to the critical role of long-standing state investment in public health infrastructure and training of PHC workers, together with extensive measures to improve geographic and economic accessibility, in achieving universal PHC. Notably, healthcare is still 'free', albeit to different extents, in all three PHC systems, with no user charges at points of service delivery. As well, financing, administration and delivery are retained, to a great extent, under government purview, although a sizeable and growing private health sector is segmenting healthcare delivery in both Sri Lanka and Thailand where the public sector remains the dominant service provider in rural areas.

All three countries have historically prioritised resources for rural health services in response to social and political exigencies beginning at distinct moments: Sri Lanka after the 1930s in response to electoral demands heightened by an epidemic of malaria and a growing left movement; Cuba following the 1959 Communist revolution; and Thailand, after the 1970s, in the context of uprisings against military regimes and medical activism. In parallel with public health infrastructure expansion in rural areas, healthcare professionals were (and are) trained locally in heavily government-subsidized diploma or degree programmes. All three PHC systems, despite seeing funding cuts over the years, are sustained by huge historic investments, and the scaffolding of people's demands and long-term expectations.

Comparing Sri Lanka's maternal and infant care service – its network of primary care facilities covering the entire country, supported by secondary and tertiary facilities, and trained professional midwives, all financed by the state – with mhealth approaches (e.g., Malawi's CCPF) reveals critical differences. With their basis in cost-efficiency, social innovation initiatives place emphasis on low-cost technologies sans substantial capital investment in public health infrastructure or recurrent expenditures on healthcare workforce training and salaries. Mhealth, based on digital technologies supported by 'partner' CSR projects, and delivered initially by (trained) 'community volunteers', is a prime example of how social innovation does little to strengthen weakened PHC systems. Far beyond health information conveyed by phone, a haemorrhaging pregnant woman must have access to PHC workers (ambulance drivers, midwives, nurses, doctors, etc.), linked to emergency obstetric care, including life-saving medicines, equipment, and infrastructure, all available free of charge in Sri Lanka.

Analogously, Thailand's policies to expand its rural workforce are vastly different from efforts to engage private drug sellers, mostly without pharmacy training, toward expanding health services in rural Uganda. The private drug shop initiative had its basis in the Ugandan Ministry of Health's iCCM strategy through which minimally trained volunteers in village health teams manage childhood fever. The innovation here was to transfer some of the iCCM costs to households via fees levied for services delivered. Training private drug sellers to diagnose and treat febrile illness in Uganda lies in stark contrast to Thailand's commitment to training and licensing nursing and paramedical professionals to manage rural health posts, in parallel with the scale-up of the VHV Programme that extends health promotion to the grassroots.

Likewise, comparison of Cuba's FDNP with OFHR's 'nurse entrepreneur' initiative highlights fundamental differences. Financed, administered, and delivered by the state, FDNP offers integrated community-oriented PHC delivered by teams of doctors, nurses, and public health practitioners, encompassing comprehensive primary care services combined with action on social and environmental determinants of health. By contrast, OFHR relies on a business model, delivering a limited 'package' of services (maternity care is excluded) and expects nurses to self-sustain themselves by generating income either through insurance claims or user charges. The sustainability (and profitability) of OFHR hinges on the income thus generated. Although initiatives like OFHR do make primary care (though not PHC) available in areas where it is lacking, they fragment existing systems, and the levies charged deter access for the desperately poor.

Beyond heath-sector investments, Sri Lanka, Thailand, and Cuba have made deep investments in rural infrastructure, including water and sanitation, education, and agriculture. Moreover, the PHC systems rely on a high degree of community engagement and participation: in Sri Lanka, public health midwives conduct home visits, health education sessions, and organise community-based health promotion activities; in Thailand, VHV, with a nominal stipend, take public health messages and health promotion activities to the grassroots; and, in Cuba, doctor-nurse teams make routine home visits and organise neighbourhood-level health promotion activities. In Thailand and Cuba, mechanisms of accountability are built into the systems via health commissions, involved in planning and evaluating PHC. Such approaches are lacking in most contemporary UHC efforts that prioritise health technologies and services in a decontextualized fashion.

The commitment in Sri Lanka, Thailand, and Cuba, to redistributive social policies, in response to electoral and other demands, both historically and contemporaneously, have enabled (at least partially) a withstanding of privatization reforms underpinned by neoliberal ideology. Because their PHC systems are sustained with little or no external/donor assistance, these countries have been able to rebuff (to some extent) reforms imposed by the World Bank and other donors. By contrast, primary care initiatives in low-income settings depend to a great extent on external actors, who fund a high proportion of overall health expenditures in these countries. A recent World Bank-commissioned study highlighted Sri Lanka's UHC achievements despite rejection of health financing reforms (Smith 2018). Thailand, too, implemented UCS against recommendations of the World Bank and IMF (Wibulpolprasert and Fleck 2014). Under a decades-long blockade, Cuba has had no dealings with international financial institutions (Pineo 2019) and implements home-grown health policies that depart from mainstream global health prescriptions.

Despite such resistance, in recent years, a steady incursion of reforms stipulating funding cuts, public sector downsizing, and privatization has plagued all three countries. In Sri Lanka, over half of total health spending transpires in the private health sector; households across the social spectrum now combine public and private maternal and infant care services. The fate of the Free Health policy remains uncertain in the face of deepening economic crisis. In Thailand, public sector reforms have curbed recruitment of healthcare cadres, including nurses, to public service, indirectly weakening rural retention policies, while medical tourism lures health workers to private sector employment and stratifies service delivery. In Cuba, recent market-oriented reforms have largely spared the health sector, but the healthcare system is pursuing efficiency through downsizing and other measures; the deteriorating economic situation may occasion further cuts. Meanwhile, increasing revenue reliance on overseas medical missions risks jeopardizing access to PHC domestically. Given the successes of these Majority World PHC alternatives and the current threats they face, it behooves global health actors to deepen understanding of, and fortify, these systems.

5 Conclusion

A corporatized vision of UHC, led by the World Bank, has long been in gestation, accelerating in recent decades with Global Health Inc.'s involvement. Corporate actors, among others, have shifted the conversation from universal *access* to *coverage*, no longer referring to comprehensive PHC within national health systems, but instead circumscribed packages of primary care services. These efforts have dovetailed with attempts to expand the private sector's role via the engagement of corporate hospital conglomerates and health insurance TNCs, even as social innovation has gained traction in some settings. Although proven examples of universal PHC systems exist, with bona fide involvement of communities, technocratic donor-led projects that have their basis in business models continue to fragment healthcare systems, normalizing starkly inferior (and racial-ized) healthcare standards for people made to live in conditions of poverty. In this last section, we review the volume's insights and end by calling for a reclaiming of truly universal public PHC systems across the Majority World.

A Corporate Vision Long in the Making

The neoliberal onslaught of the 1980s, and the US's disempowering of WHO, enabled the World Bank to emerge as a formidable force shaping global health. Guided by the Bank's 1980s framework for public–private financing of health services, SALs introduced cost-recovery measures to sustain health systems beleaguered by funding cuts. The World Bank modified its approach in the 1990s, framing health as an investment opportunity, and proposing a state-financed essential services package that has endured to this day. 'Pluralistic' delivery within mixed systems became the standard based on the assumption that the private health sector was indispensable in LMICs. And the Bank's calls for heightened public financing, in parallel with governments opening health-care markets for domestic and foreign investment, transformed healthcare systems into profitable business ventures subsidized by governments.

A set of corporate actors, some pre-existing, some new, became increasingly involved in global health at the turn of the millennium. The BMGF's influence and its preoccupation with digital technologies, entrepreneurship, and innovation transformed the field, resetting priorities and practices in global health (Birn and Richter 2018; Martens and Seitz 2015; Wiist 2011). Consequently, UHC became heavily influenced by business logics and increasingly profit-driven (Wagner-Rizvi 2020). Overshadowing the principle of universality and the desirability of a single level of care, corporate rhetoric and approaches manifested at WHO, a clear example being the discourse of 'new universalism', meaning 'coverage for all, not coverage of everything' (WHO 1999). Further, the language of 'sustain-ability' normalised cost-sharing, requiring service users to pay.

Under Global Health Inc.'s influence, the 'purchaser-provider split' was hailed as a mechanism to enhance the efficiency and quality of (public) health-care, gaining widespread acceptance in health reform efforts (Smithers and Waitzkin 2022). National health insurance schemes that involved mixed public and private financing proliferated in the Majority World, enabling governments to limit service packages. These insurance schemes typically comprised mul-tiple pooled funds, covering wildly different service packages and segmenting healthcare delivery (Birn et al. 2016; Fenny et al. 2021). Since the 1990s, financialization has profoundly shaped health financing reforms (Hunter and Murray 2019), amplified by the World Bank's (1993) calls for removal of protections enjoyed by domestic suppliers of health products and services (Sell 2019). The lucrative nature of UHC has moved corporate giants like KPMG to establish UHC consulting services to assist governments to reorganize PHC systems (KPMG 2022), while private investment in healthcare increasingly involves speculative financing, subject to fewer regulations, more risk (borne by governments) and boundless profits (Stein and Sridhar 2018).

Building on this trajectory, current approaches to UHC are informed by Global Health Inc.'s vision: to expand access to (and markets for) health technologies, products, and services (see WHO 2023), unlike comprehensive PHC that demands attention to the social, economic, and political factors shaping health. The focus on primary care (as opposed to PHC) has enabled this diversion, with the social determinants of health only fleetingly mentioned in the 2010 WHR, 2018 Astana Declaration, and the UN's 2019 Political Declaration. Requiring expansive redistributive measures, along the lines of those described in Section 4, the social and environmental determinants of health are usually placed on the backburner by governments and donors alike. Indeed, donor-driven initiatives overwhelmingly focus on 'magic bullets', namely vaccines, medicines, or health products like insecticide-treated bed nets, among others (Birn et al. 2017).

At bottom, social innovation approaches, while extending a limited form of primary care (distinguished from PHC) in underserved low-income settings, also expand markets for health technologies, products, and services. Those described in Section 3 create business opportunities for the digital technologies industry, Big Pharma, and franchisers, while offloading the burden of healthcare financing to households, even as their donors would have secured tax exemptions. A myriad such UHC projects channel funds towards private profit, weakening and fragmenting healthcare systems across the Majority World. Even so, these approaches are normalised, accepted, and even hailed, by dominant global health actors, with little regard for their implications for health systems in Majority World settings and peoples' access to healthcare.

Dehumanized Places and Peoples

Traced back to the first International Sanitary Conference held in Paris (1851), modern international health efforts focused on curbing epidemics that imperilled trade and labour productivity. With the entry of the Rockefeller Foundation in the early twentieth-century, the interplay of state responsibility for public health and the impetus for global capitalism spurred efforts to advance international health, albeit favouring shorter-term technical disease-control approaches, over longer-term support of political and social redistribution in colonised territories

(Birn et al. 2017). Deriving from these legacies, global health initiatives today align with business and naturalize inferior racialized health system standards for people living in the (mostly Black and Brown) Majority World (Chaudhuri et al. 2021; Kwete et al. 2022).

Even the Alma-Ata Declaration, despite its progressive underpinnings, did not herald a single level of (comprehensive) care for all, but rather PHC that is affordable to the country and community (WHO 1978). The selective PHC approach grew from a proposal for five low-cost interventions for women and children (Walsh and Warren 1979), concretised in the World Bank-backed essential services package that has persisted since the 1990s and informs UHC today. With little regard for ethics, not to mention the racialized underpinnings of their interventions, dominant global health actors collude with local elites to define, based on cost-effectiveness, scanty primary care service packages, often associated with user-fees or other forms of cost recovery.

As such, the scope and quality of UHC envisioned for the Majority World is limited. To be sure, the inadequacy of resources, following centuries of colonial pillage and extractivism, is taken as given and rarely questioned on ethical grounds. In fact, there seems to be wide consensus that universal and comprehensive PHC is simply not feasible in LICs. Patchy social innovation-driven primary care approaches are preferred on the grounds of cost-efficiency. As we saw in Section 3, private drug sellers, without pharmacy qualifications, were cursorily trained to diagnose and treat childhood febrile illness based on globally applicable iCCM protocols, rather than building a cadre of primary care workers to undertake this work. Indeed, task shifting is frequently invoked to enlist the services of inadequately qualified laypersons, often unpaid, in lieu of salaried health workers. That said, community health workers do in fact undertake crucial work in countries with strong PHC systems. However, they undergo thorough training in organized programmes, and are integrated into the healthcare system. In Thailand, VHV deliver health promotion interventions and basic care, supervised by licensed primary care workers, who also serve as conduits providing additional expertise and referral when needed (Pongpirul 2020). Levying fees is also naturalised in the name of sustainability amid desperately low levels of health system funding, the latter often channelled towards donor-prioritised health problems/areas.

A bigger problem is that these piecemeal primary care initiatives are driven by other agendas. Bilateral agencies and philanthropies shroud their largely foreign policy and pro-market interventions in the language of humanitarianism (BMGF (1991–2023); USAID n.d.). Sidestepping any discussion of reparations or health justice, their efforts have resulted in a long-lasting form of disaster capitalism (Klein 2007), particularly in Sub-Saharan African countries, where a large proportion of health financing is externally financed by donors. As the latter have considerable influence on agenda-setting, these conditions provide fertile ground for testing and implementing externally-driven solutions for public health problems. Hatched in the minds of 'entrepreneurs', almost invariably external to the context, social innovations of unproven efficacy are rolled out absent accountability (Fejerskov 2017). Given their circumscribed nature, they represent 'crumbs for the poor', providing band-aid solutions that are unlikely to result in long-lasting systemic change.

Role of Government

Since the 1970s the US and its allies have lobbied against assigning responsibility for healthcare delivery to governments (Litsios 2002). A half-century later, WHO offers little guidance on the role of governments in healthcare delivery, except to say that they should provide stewardship in the governance of mixed public–private systems (WHO 2010a, 2020a). Ministries of health in particular are portrayed as bureaucratic, corrupt, and incompetent (WHO CMH 2001), fostering widespread perception and acceptance of the notion that (LMIC) governments are incapable of delivering universal healthcare (Ruckert and Labonte 2014).

Relatedly, the World Bank obfuscates the notion of universality by incessantly and misleadingly arguing that universal and free (at the point of use) healthcare systems give rise to inequity. If governments provide universal access at a single level of care, the Bank contends, the wealthy will benefit disproportionately – for services they can finance through private channels – thereby widening inequity. Directing the better off to private facilities, as per the World Bank formula, has led to a proliferation of two- or multi-tiered healthcare systems, with segmentation of services between rich and poor, unionized and non-unionized, and urban and rural populations in many Majority World settings (Birn et al. 2016, 2017). By contrast, Cuba's highly effective publicly financed, administered, and delivered healthcare system, which has made great strides towards health equity, is disregarded by the World Bank, UN and even WHO (Cooper et al. 2006), along with any acknowledgement of the state-dominant character of Sri Lanka's and Thailand's healthcare systems. Ultimately, the World Bank's prophecy that universal health systems would unduly benefit the rich has been realized, not through public healthcare systems but through UHC, which sees public financing and profit channelled to the pockets of Global Health Inc.

In the PHC settings described in Section 4, large-scale redistribution was crucial to advancing health equity. Responding to claims on the state made by citizens, these countries implemented policies that involved transfer of resources from rich to poor, curative to preventive services, and scale-up of rural services to the standard and density of urban counterparts. In addition to prioritizing infrastructure expansion (especially in rural areas) in the early stages, these PHC initiatives emphasized programmes to train and retain skilled health workers. Most striking is that in all three countries, PHC initiatives were, at the time of their launching, embedded within larger programmes of rural development, targeting improvements in water, sanitation, nutrition, employment, and, importantly, education – decades prior to the recommendations of the WHO Commission on Social Determinants of Health. Moreover, such large-scale social investments also contributed towards addressing gender disparities, particularly in health and education (Perera et al. 2022).

Governments must play a key role in healthcare delivery to maintain universality and drive costs down. Thailand's retention of UCS purchasing in the public sector enabled the government to engage in monopsonistic purchasing and procure medicines according to a National Essential Medicines List, generating huge savings for the healthcare system (Tangcharoensathien et al. 2018; WHO 2015). In Sri Lanka, the government has been able to control healthcare costs by purveying the bulk of healthcare delivery with half of total health spending (Amarasinghe at al. 2015). Still, these systems have been unable to withstand privatization exigencies. The healthcare system in Sri Lanka is crumbling under economic crisis, and Thailand's UCS scheme is under strain. In Cuba too, public sector restructuring is ongoing. Affecting all three settings, the poaching of locally trained physicians and health workers by the West continues unabated.

The Remaking of Universal Health

Amid the Covid-19 pandemic, a World Bank (2021) report, *Walking the Talk: Reimagining Primary Health Care After COVID-19*, recommended three strategies to advance PHC: multi-disciplinary team-based care (with empanelment)[7], a multi-professional health workforce, and public financing for PHC (*free* at the point-of-care). Even so, the Bank steadfastly advocated a mixed public–private model of primary care, despite obscene profiteering by for-profit providers and yawning Big Pharma-led vaccine inequities in the pandemic setting (Hunter et al. 2022; Pilkington et al. 2022). In April 2022, the Lancet Global Health Commission on Financing Primary Health Care similarly endorsed publicly financed primary care packages within mixed public–private systems (Hanson et al. 2022). Neither entity mentioned the troubling fallout of private sector engagement or the missing crucial ingredient: *public delivery*.

---

[7] Empanelment refers to the process and system of identifying and assigning people to specific healthcare providers or teams for primary care.

Despite the obstinate and relentless support for mixed public–private health-care systems (notwithstanding questionable if not absent evidence), there is apparent consensus between the World Bank and Lancet Commission for far-reaching reforms involving investment in PHC systems and health workers in the post-Covid era. While even mainstream global health players seem to recognize that the pandemic has demonstrated need for radical change, most fail to regret their predecessors' backing of baseless policies, including user-fees, means-testing, demand-side financing, social innovations, and other piece-meal interventions that have weakened public systems in the Majority World. The present trajectory of increasing public financing *sans* delivery will not work. The current WHO Director-General has flagged rising out-of-pocket spending, despite 'coverage' improvements in recent years (WHO 2023), and mainstream analysts project increasing out-of-pocket expenditures on health over the next two decades in low- and lower-middle income countries (Dieleman et al. 2018). Healthcare financing and delivery options that are equitable, just, and affordable (for governments *and* people) are the need of the hour, and must be reflected in UHC indicators, which currently mask the distinction between public and private.

The PHC initiatives in Sri Lanka, Thailand, and Cuba emerged from socio-political struggles. Although WHO (2010a) acknowledges the political nature of health reform and the need to move away from cookie-cutter approaches, UHC initiatives are, by and large, technocratic interventions divorced from people's struggles. In perusing the case studies of social innovation on the SIHI website, we found that 'local' usually referred to NGOs based in LICs, and not the communities supposedly served by the innovations. By contrast, the PHC systems of Thailand and Cuba involve the communities served through Health Assemblies and Popular Councils, respectively. Unless the political and con-tested nature of health reform is recognized, and reform initiatives are led by governments with bona fide peoples' involvement, long-lasting and systemic change may never take place.

At the core of global health is a double standard that has endured since colonial times. Given the elite makeup of the global health establishment, its decision-makers, regardless of country of origin, remain distant from the intended beneficiaries of global health initiatives. This distance makes it pos-sible to adjudicate the cost-effectiveness of interventions and define limited service packages or health technologies for those made-marginalized, even as the decision-makers live in opulence, jetting across the world. Pointedly, global health elites can refrain from asking themselves whether they would be satisfied with consulting a community health worker by phone during an obstetric emergency or a minimally trained private drug seller about their child's fever.

For this, among myriad reasons, calls to decolonize global health ought not to be limited to concerns of epistemology and representation, but should also address the need to radically democratise power and resources (Chaudhuri et al. 2021; Kwete et al. 2022).

The terms of global health debates regarding UHC, with funding and frameworks furnished by bilateral and multilateral agencies and private philanthropies, mean a privileging of certain kinds of values and epistemologies, which in turn shape global health practices (Chaudhuri et al. 2021). This means reliance on 'data-driven' or 'evidence-based' solutions narrowly conceptualized without accounting for aspects that are difficult to measure or unfold over long periods. It also means prioritizing 'cost-effective' health technologies, even where the most basic public health infrastructure, including water, sanitation, healthcare facilities, and workers, are lacking. For instance, today, global health funders prioritize mhealth (and increasingly artificial intelligence – AI), with little regard for what is really needed 'on the ground'. Global Health Inc.'s influence at UN agencies (including WHO) and universities drives the emphasis on entrepreneurship and innovation, overlooking the social justice-oriented goals of global public health.

How might control be wrested from Global Health Inc.? A common theme across Sri Lanka, Thailand, and Cuba is rejection of neoliberal policies in health, despite World Bank and IMF pressures. It was strong public support that moved these PHC systems in progressive directions, even and especially amid economic crisis. Thus, a necessary first step is for people everywhere to rally public support for redistributive social policies, and demand that political parties take forward social justice-oriented health agendas. The 'Public' must be seized from the grasp of shareholders and profit-seekers, in order to fulfil peoples' expressed needs and solidarity-based aspirations for health.

Abbreviations

ACT	artemisinin-based combination therapy
AIDS	acquired immunodeficiency syndrome
AMFm	Affordable Medicines Facility-Malaria
BMGF	Bill and Melinda Gates Foundation
CBHI	community-based health insurance
CCPF	Chipatala Cha Pa Foni
CHAM	Christian Health Association of Malawi
CMH	Commission on Macroeconomics and Health
CPIPRD	Collaborative Project to Increase Production of Rural Doctors
CSDOH	Commission on Social Determinants of Health
CSMB	Civil Servants Medical Benefits Scheme
CSR	corporate social responsibility
DALY	disability-adjusted life year
DPT	diphtheria, pertussis, and tetanus
FDNP	Family Doctor and Nurse Programme
FHSDC	Financing health services in developing countries
G77	Group of 77
GDP	gross domestic product
GNI	gross national income
GSK	GlaxoSmithKline
HiAP	Health in all policies
HIC	high-income countries
HIV	human immunodeficiency virus
iCCM	Integrated community case management
IDRC	International Development Research Centre
IMF	International Monetary Fund
LIC	low-income countries
LMIC	low- and middle-income countries
MIC	middle-income countries
MOH	medical officer of health
NCD	non-communicable diseases
NGO	non-governmental organisation
NHSO	National Health Security Office
NIEO	New International Economic Order
ODOD	One District One Doctor Programme
OECD	Organisation for Economic Co-operation and Development

OFHR	One Family Health Rwanda
ORS	oral rehydration salts
PEPFAR	President's Emergency Plan for AIDS Relief
PHC	primary healthcare
PPP	public–private partnership
RDT	rapid diagnostic test
SAL	structural adjustment loan
SDG	sustainable development goal
SHI	social health insurance
SIHI	Social Innovations in Health Initiative
SPHC	selective primary healthcare
TDR	Special Programme for Research and Training in Tropical Diseases
TNC	transnational company
TRIPS	Trade Related Aspects of Intellectual Property Rights
UCS	Universal Coverage Scheme
UHC	universal health coverage
UK	United Kingdom
UN	United Nations
UNCTAD	United Nations Conference on Trade and Development
UNDP	United Nations Development Programme
UNFPA	United Nations Population Fund
US	United States of America
USAID	United States Agency for International Development
USD	United States Dollar
USSR	Union of Soviet Socialist Republics
VHV	village health volunteers
WBTI	World Breast Feeding Trends Initiative
WDR	World development report
WHA	World Health Assembly
WHO	World Health Organization
WHR	World health report

References

Al Dahdah, M. (2022). Between philanthropy and big business: The rise of mHealth in the global health market. *Development and Change, 53*, 376–95. https://doi.org/10.1111/dech.12497.

Amarasinghe, S., De Alwis, S., Saleem, S., Rannan-Eliya, R. P., & Dalpatadu, S. (2015). *Private health sector review 2012*. Institute for Health Policy, Colombo. www.ihp.lk/publications/docs/PHSR2012.pdf.

Anand, S. & Hanson, K. (1997). Disability-adjusted life years: A critical review. *Journal of Health Economics, 16*(6), 685–702. https://doi.org/10.1016/S0167-6296(97)00005-2.

Armstrong, P., Amaratunga, C., & Bernier, J. Grant, K., Pederson, A. & Willson, K. (2001). *Exposing privatization: Women and health care reform in Canada*. Ontario: Garamond Press.

Arora, R., Chamnan, P., Nitiapinyasakul, A., & Lertsukprasert, S. (2017). Retention of doctors in rural health services in Thailand: Impact of a national collaborative approach. *Rural and Remote Health, 17*(3), 1–10. https://doi.org/10.22605/RRH4344.

Awor, P., Kalyango, J. N., Stålsby Lundborg, C. et al. (2022). Policy challenges facing the scale up of integrated community case management (iCCM) in Uganda. *International Journal of Health Policy and Management, 11*(8), 1432–41. https://dx.doi.org/10.34172/ijhpm.2021.39.

Awor, P., Wamani, H., Bwire, G., Jagoe, G., & Peterson, S. (2012). Private sector drug shops in integrated community case management of malaria, pneumonia, and diarrhea in children in Uganda. *The American Journal of Tropical Medicine and Hygiene, 87*(5_Suppl), 92–6. https://doi.org/10.4269/ajtmh.2012.11-0791.

Awor, P., Wamani, H., Tylleskar, T., Jagoe, G., & Peterson, S. (2014). Increased access to care and appropriateness of treatment at private sector drug shops with integrated management of malaria, pneumonia and diarrhoea: A quasi-experimental study in Uganda. *PLoS One, 9*(12), e115440. https://doi.org/10.1371/journal.pone.0115440.

Awor, P., Wamani, H., Tylleskar, T., & Peterson, S. (2015). Drug seller adherence to clinical protocols with integrated management of malaria, pneumonia and diarrhoea at drug shops in Uganda. *Malaria Journal, 14*(1), 1–6. https://doi.org/10.1186/s12936-015-0798-9.

Ayal, E. B. (1962). Thailand's six-year National Economic Development Plan. *Asian Survey, 1*(11), 33–42. https://doi.org/10.2307/3023638.

Bagchi, A. (2022). Neoliberal turn in the domain of health care: The emergence of corporate health care sector in India. In A. Chatterjee and N. Chatterjee, eds., *Covid-19 in India, disease, health and culture*. Oxon: Routledge, pp. 117–33.

Bagonza, A., Peterson, S., & Mårtensson, A. et al. (2020). Regulatory inspection of registered private drug shops in East-Central Uganda – What it is versus what it should be: A qualitative study. *Journal of Pharmaceutical Policy and Practice*, *13*(1), 1–11. https://doi.org/10.1186/s40545-020-00265-9.

Baru, R. V. (2003). Privatisation of health services: A South Asian perspective. *Economic and Political Weekly*, *38*(42), 4433–7.

Becker, H. (2021). The impact of the COVID-19 global pandemic on the Cuban tourism industry and recommendations for Cuba's response. *Multidisciplinary Business Review*, *14*(1), 71–83. https://doi.org/10.35692/07183992.14.1.7.

Birn, A. E. (2014a). Backstage: The relationship between the rockefeller foundation and the world health organization, part I: 1940s–1960s. *Public Health*, **128**(2), 129–40. https://doi.org/10.1016/j.puhe.2013.11.010.

Birn, A. E. (2014b). Philanthrocapitalism, past and present: The rockefeller foundation, the gates foundation, and the setting (s) of the international/global health agenda. *Hypothesis*, *12*(1), e8. https://doi.org/10.5779/hypothesis.v12i1.229.

Birn, A. E., & Hellander, I. (2016). Market-driven health care mess: The United States. *Cadernos De Saude Publica*, *32*(3). https://doi.org/10.1590/0102-311X00014816.

Birn, A. E., & Krementsov, N. (2018). 'Socialising' primary care? The Soviet Union, WHO and the 1978 Alma-Ata Conference. *BMJ Global Health*, *3*(Suppl 3), e000992. https://doi.org/10.1136/bmjgh-2018-000992.

Birn, A. E., & Nervi, L. (2019). What matters in health (care) universes: Delusions, dilutions, and ways towards universal health justice. *Globalization and Health*, *15*(1), 1–12. https://doi.org/10.1186/s12992-019-0521-7.

Birn, A. E., Nervi, L., & Siqueira, E. (2016). Neoliberalism redux: The global health policy agenda and the politics of cooptation in Latin America and beyond. *Development and Change*, *47*(4), 734–59. https://doi.org/10.1111/dech.12247.

Birn, A. E., Pillay, Y., & Holtz, T. H. (2017). *Textbook of global health*. New York: Oxford University Press.

Birn, A. E., & Richter, J. (2018). Health care under the knife: Moving beyond capitalism for our health. In Howard Waitzkin and the Working Group on

Health Beyond Capitalism, eds., *US Philanthrocapitalism and the global health agenda: The Rockefeller and Gates foundations, past and present*, pp. 155–74. New York: Monthly Review Press.

Birn, A. E., Zimmerman, S., & Garfield, R. (2000). To decentralize or not to decentralize, is that the question? Nicaraguan health policy under structural adjustment in the 1990s. *International Journal of Health Services, 30*(1), 111–28. https://doi.org/10.2190/C6TB-B16Y-60HV-M3QW.

Birungi, H., Mugisha, F., Nsabagasani, X., Okuonzi, S., & Jeppsson, A. (2001). The policy on public–private mix in the Ugandan health sector: Catching up with reality. *Health Policy and Planning, 16*(suppl 2), 80–7. https://doi.org/10.1093/heapol/16.suppl_2.80.

Blauvelt, C., West, M., Maxim, L. et al. (2018). Scaling up a health and nutrition hotline in Malawi: The benefits of multisectoral collaboration. *British Medical Journal, 363*, k4590. https://doi.org/10.1136/bmj.k4590.

BMGF (1991–2023). Our story. www.gatesfoundation.org/about/our-story.

Breakthrough RESEARCH and VillageReach (2021). *Chipatala cha pa Foni, Malawi's "Health Center by Phone", improving information given about pregnancy-related symptoms, APPHC Case Study*. Washington, DC: Population Council. https://breakthroughactionandresearch.org/wp-content/uploads/2021/05/BR_APPHC_CaseStudy_CCPF.pdf.

Brotherton, P. S. (2013). Fueling la revolución: Itinerant physicians, transactional humanitarianism, and shifting moral economies in post-Soviet Cuba. In N. J. Burke, ed., *Health travels: Cuban health(care) on and off the Island*. San Francisco: University of California Medical Humanities Press, pp.129–53.

Campion, E. W., & Morrissey, S. (2013). A different model: Medical care in Cuba. *The New England Journal of Medicine, 368*(4), 297. https://doi.org/10.1056/NEJMp1215226.

Cardenas, L. T. G., Mejias, L. C., Perea, L. P. et al. (2018). The Family Doctor and Nurse Program: Development of the health care model in Cuba. *Pan American Journal of Public Health, 42*, 1. https://doi.org/10.26633/RPSP.2018.31.

Castillo, N. M., & Vosloo, S. (2017). *Chipatala cha pa Foni (CCPF): Case study by UNESCO-Pearson initiative for literacy.* https://unesdoc.unesco.org/ark:/48223/pf0000258875.

Chansa, C., & Pattnaik, A. (2018). *Expanding health care provision in a low-income country: The experience of Malawi.* Universal Health Coverage Study Series No. 34. World Bank Group, Washington, D.C. https://open

knowledge.worldbank.org/server/api/core/bitstreams/6ac2d590-f698-5e25-8106-007344aa31fe/content.

Charles, L., Moe, J., & Bartlett, R. (2013). *One Family Health Rwanda: Achievements and challenges* 2012. www.innovationsinhealthcare.org/OFH %20Case%20Study%20FINAL.pdf.

Charuluxananan, S., & Chentanez, V. (2007). History and evolution of western medicine in Thailand. *Asian Biomedicine, 1*(1), 97–101.

Chaudhuri, M. M., Mkumba, L., Raveendran, Y., & Smith, R. D. (2021). Decolonising global health: Beyond 'reformative' roadmaps and towards decolonial thought. *BMJ Global Health, 6*(7), e006371. http://dx.doi.org/10.1136/bmjgh-2021-006371.

Chemouni, B. (2018). The political path to universal health coverage: Power, ideas and community-based health insurance in Rwanda. *World Development, 106*, 87–98. https://doi.org/10.1016/j.worlddev.2018.01.023.

Chorev, N. (2012). *The World Health Organization between north and south.* Ithaca, NY: Cornell University Press.

Christensen, C. M. (1997). *The innovator's dilemma: When new technologies cause great firms to fail.* Boston, MA: Harvard Business School Press.

Christensen, C. M., Baumann, H., Ruggles, R., & Sadtler, T. M. (2006). Disruptive innovation for social change. *Harvard Business Review, 84*(12), 94.

Cooper, R. S., Kennelly, J. F., & Ordunez-Garcia, P. (2006). Health in Cuba. *International Journal of Epidemiology, 35*(4), 817–24. https://doi.org/10.1093/ije/dyl175.

Cueto, M. (2004). The origins of primary health care and selective primary health care. *American Journal of Public Health, 94*(11), 1864–74. https://doi.org/10.2105/AJPH.94.11.1864.

Cueto, M., Brown, T. M., & Fee, E. (2019). *The World Health Organization: A history.* Cambridge: Cambridge University Press.

Daily FT (2020). World Bank downgrades SL to lower-middle income country, *Daily FT,* 3 July 2020. www.ft.lk/Front-Page/World-Bank-downgrades-SL-to-lower-middle-income-country/44-702511.

Daniel, S. (2016). Why Sri Lanka beats India in maternal mortality ratios? *Al Jazeera,* 14 March 2016. www.aljazeera.com/features/2016/3/14/why-sri-lanka-beats-india-in-maternal-mortality-ratios.

Department of Census and Statistics Sri Lanka (2017). *Demographic and health survey 2016.* www.statistics.gov.lk/Health/StaticalInformation/Demographic AndHealthSurvey-2016FullReport.

De Silva, D. (2017). How many doctors should we train for Sri Lanka? System dynamics modelling for training needs. *Ceylon Medical Journal, 62*(4), 233–7. https://doi.org/10.4038/cmj.v62i4.8573.

De Vos, P. (2019). Cuba's strategy toward universal health. *International Journal of Health Services*, *49*(1), 186–92. https://doi.org/10.1177/002073141 8804406.

Dieleman, J. L., Sadat, N., Chang, A. Y. et al. (2018). Trends in future health financing and coverage: Future health spending and universal health coverage in 188 countries, 2016–40. *The Lancet*, *391*(10132), 1783–98. https://doi .org/10.1016/S0140-6736(18)30697-4.

Djukanovic, V., & Mach, E. P. (1975). *Alternative approaches to meeting basic health needs in developing countries: A joint UNICEF/WHO study*. https:// apps.who.int/iris/handle/10665/40076.

Doshi, P. P., Bhosai, S. J., Goldmann, D., & Udayakumar, K. (2021). Imagining the future of primary care: A global look at innovative health care delivery. *NEJM Catalyst Innovations in Care Delivery*, *2*(1). https://catalyst.nejm.org/ doi/full/10.1056/CAT.20.0481

Duke Innovation and Entrepreneurship (2022). *Changing the world through entrepreneurial action*. https://entrepreneurship.duke.edu/.

Emmanuel, M. (2019). *The impact of restructuring on public sector performance: A case study of RSSB/CBHI*. MBA Research Thesis, University of Rwanda. http://154.68.126.42/bitstream/handle/123456789/940/MUGABO .pdf?sequence=1&isAllowed=y.

Epstein, G. (2005) *Financialization and the world economy*. Cheltenham: Edward Elgar.

Family Health Bureau (2021). *Annual report of the Family Health Bureau 2019*. Colombo, Sri Lanka: Ministry of Health. https://fhb.health.gov.lk/index.php/ en/resources/annual-report.

Farris, S. R., & Marchetti, S. (2017). From the commodification to the corporatization of care: European perspectives and debates. *Social Politics: International Studies in Gender, State & Society*, *24*(2), 109–31. https://doi .org/10.1093/sp/jxx003.

Fejerskov, A. M. (2017). The new technopolitics of development and the global south as a laboratory of technological experimentation. *Science, Technology, & Human Values*, *42*(5), 947–68. https://doi.org/10.1177/01622439177 09934.

Fenny, A. P., Yates, R., & Thompson, R. (2021). Strategies for financing social health insurance schemes for providing universal health care: A comparative analysis of five countries. *Global Health Action*, *14*(1), 1868054. https://doi .org/10.1080/16549716.2020.1868054.

Fernandez, A. F. T. (1975). The national health system in Cuba. In K. W. Newell, ed., *Health by the people*, pp. 13–29. Geneva: WHO. https:// apps.who.int/iris/handle/10665/40514.

Fine, B., & Saad Filho, A. (2014). Politics of neoliberal development: Washington Consensus and post-Washington Consensus. In H. Weber, ed., *The politics of development: A survey*. Milton Park: Routledge, pp. 154–66.

Fukuda-Parr, S., & Hulme, D. (2011). International norm dynamics and the end of poverty: Understanding the millennium development goals. *Global Governance*, *17*, 17–36. https://doi.org/10.1163/19426720-01701002.

G77 (1989). *Caracas declaration of the Ministers of Foreign Affairs of the Group of 77 on the occasion of the twenty-fifth anniversary of the Group* (Caracas, Venezuela, 21–23 June 1989). www.g77.org/doc/A-44-361-E.pdf.

Garfield, R., & Santana, S. (1997). The impact of the economic crisis and the US embargo on health in Cuba. *American Journal of Public Health*, *87*(1), 15–20. https://doi.org/10.2105/AJPH.87.1.15.

Glackin, J. P. (n.d.). *What exactly is a L3C?* Boston College Legal Services Lab. http://bclawlab.org/eicblog/2017/3/21/what-exactly-is-a-l3c.

Global Grand Challenges (2003–23). *Global grand challenges*. https://gcgh .grandchallenges.org/.

Global Health Watch (2017). *Global Health Watch 5: An alternative world health report*. London: Zed Books.

Gonzalez, A. M. G., Lopez, R. G., Muniz, M. A. et al. (2018). Economic considerations on Cuban public health and its relationship with universal health. *Revista Panamericana de Salud Publica*, *42*(1). https://doi.org/ 10.26633/RPSP.2018.28.

Gosling, D. (1985). Thailand's bare-headed doctors. *Modern Asian Studies*, *19*(4), 761–96. https://doi.org/10.1017/S0026749X00015468.

Government of Malawi (2016). *Malawi Demographic and Health Survey 2015-16 key indicators report*. www.healthynewbornnetwork.org/hnn-content/ uploads/Malawi-DHS-2015-2016-KIR-Final-05-27-2016.pdf.

Guenther, T., Nsona, H., Makuluni, R. et al. (2019). Home visits by community health workers for pregnant mothers and newborns: Coverage plateau in Malawi. *Journal of Global Health*, *9*(1). https://doi.org/10.7189/jogh.09.01 0808.

Halpaap, B., Peeling, R. W., & Bonnici, F. (2019). The role of multilateral organizations and governments in advancing social innovation in health care delivery. *Infectious Diseases of Poverty*, *8*(1), 1–5. https://doi.org/10.1186/ s40249-019-0592-y.

Halpaap, B. M., Tucker, J. D., Mathanga, D. et al. (2020). Social innovation in global health: Sparking location action. *The Lancet Global Health*, *8*(5), e633–4. https://doi.org/10.1016/S2214-109X(20)30070-X.

Halstead, S. B., Walsh, J. A., & Warren, K. S. (1985). *Good health at low cost*. New York: Rockefeller Foundation.

Hanson, K., Brikci, N., Erlangga, D. et al. (2022). The Lancet Global Health Commission on financing primary health care: Putting people at the centre. *The Lancet Global Health*, *10*(5), e715–2. https://doi.org/10.1016/S2214-109X(22)00005-5.

Harris, J. (2017). *Achieving access: Professional movements and the politics of health universalism*. Ithaca: Cornell University Press.

Harris, J., & Libardi Maia, J. (2022). Universal healthcare does not look the same everywhere: Divergent experiences with the private sector in Brazil and Thailand. *Global Public Health*, *17*(9), 1809–26. https://doi.org/10.1080/17441692.2021.1981973.

Harvey, D. (2005). *A brief history of neoliberalism*. Oxford: Oxford University Press.

Haththotuwa, R., Senanayake, L., Senarath, U., & Attygalle, D. (2012). Models of care that have reduced maternal mortality and morbidity in Sri Lanka. *International Journal of Gynecology & Obstetrics*, *119*, S45–S49. https://doi.org/10.1016/j.ijgo.2012.03.016.

Hemas Hospitals (2022). *Baby delivery.* https://hemashospitals.com/services/thalawathugoda/baby-delivery/.

Hewa, S. (1995). *Colonialism, tropical disease, and imperial medicine: Rockefeller philanthropy in Sri Lanka*. Lanham, MD: University Press of America.

Hewa, S. (2011). Sri Lanka's Health Unit program: A model of 'selective' primary health care. *Hygiea Internationalis*, *10*(2), 7–33. https://doi.org/10.3384/HYGIEA.1403-8668.111027.

Holmlund, S., Ntaganira, J., Edvardsson, K. et al. (2017). Improved maternity care if midwives learn to perform ultrasound: A qualitative study of Rwandan midwives' experiences and views of obstetric ultrasound. *Global Health Action*, *10*(1), 1350451. https://doi.org/10.1080/16549716.2017.1350451.

Hunter, B. M., & Murray, S. F. (2019). Deconstructing the financialization of healthcare. *Development and Change*, *50*(5), 1263–87. https://doi.org/10.1111/dech.12517.

Hunter, D. J., Abdool Karim, S. S., Baden, L. R. et al. (2022). Addressing vaccine inequity – Covid-19 vaccines as a global public good. *New England Journal of Medicine*, **386**(12), 1176–9. https://doi.org/10.1056/NEJMe2202547.

Institute for Health Policy (2021). *Sri Lanka health accounts: National health expenditure 1990–2019*. http://ihp.lk/publications/docs/HES2106.pdf.

Jones, M. (2002). Infant and maternal health services in Ceylon, 1900–1948: Imperialism or welfare? *Social History of Medicine*, *15*(2), 263–89. https://doi.org/10.1093/shm/15.2.263.

Kalapurakkel, S. (2021). *Achieving value: A case study of the One Family Health care delivery model in the context of Rwanda's vision for universal health coverage.* Master's Thesis, Duke University. https://hdl.handle.net/10161/23323.

Kantamaturapoj, K., Marshall, A. I., Chotchoungchatchai, S. et al. (2020). Performance of Thailand's universal health coverage scheme: Evaluating the effectiveness of annual public hearings. *Health Expectations*, **23**(6), 1594–602. https://doi.org/10.1111/hex.13142.

Keck, C. W., & Reed, G. A. (2012). The curious case of Cuba. *American Journal of Public Health*, **102**(8), e13–e22. https://doi.org/10.2105/AJPH.2012 .300822.

Khan, T., Abimbola, S., Kyobutungi, C., & Pai, M. (2022). How we classify countries and people – and why it matters. *BMJ Global Health*, 7(6), e009704. http://dx.doi.org/10.1136/bmjgh-2022-009704.

Kirk, J. M. (2015). *Healthcare without borders: Understanding Cuban medical internationalism.* Gainesville: University Press of Florida.

Kitutu, F. E., Kalyango, J. N., Mayora, C. et al. (2017). Integrated community case management by drug sellers influences appropriate treatment of paediatric febrile illness in South Western Uganda: A quasi-experimental study. *Malaria Journal*, **16**(1), 1–18. https://doi.org/10.1186/s12936-017-2072-9.

Klein, N. (2007). *The shock doctrine: The rise of disaster capitalism.* New York: Henry Holt.

Konde-Lule, J., Gitta, S. N., Lindfors, A. et al. (2010). Private and public health care in rural areas of Uganda. *BMC International Health and Human Rights*, **10**(1), 1–8. https://doi.org/10.1186/1472-698X-10-29.

KPMG (2022). *KPMG centre for universal health coverage.* https://home .kpmg/xx/en/home/industries/healthcare/kpmg-center-for-universal-health-coverage.html.

Kruk, M. E., Porignon, D., Rockers, P. C., & Van Lerberghe, W. (2010). The contribution of primary care to health and health systems in low-and middle-income countries: A critical review of major primary care initiatives. *Social Science & Medicine*, **70**(6), 904–11. https://doi.org/ 10.1016/j.socscimed.2009.11.025.

Kumar, R. (2019). Public–private partnerships for universal health coverage? The future of 'free health' in Sri Lanka. *Globalization and Health*, **15**(1), 1–10. https://doi.org/10.1186/s12992-019-0522-6.

Kumar, R. (2020). *Antenatal care service utilization in public and private sectors, out-of-pocket payments, and associated factors among 'low risk' pregnant women awaiting delivery at a public sector maternity centre in Colombo.* Master's Thesis, University of Colombo.

Kumar, R. (2022). Brain drain and future of medical education. *The Island*, November 22. https://island.lk/brain-drain-and-future-of-medical-education/.

Kumar, R., Birn, A. E., Bhuyan, R., & Wong, J. P. H. (2022). Universal health coverage and public-private arrangements within Sri Lanka's mixed health system: Perspectives from women seeking healthcare. *Social Science & Medicine*, *296*, 114777. https://doi.org/10.1016/j.socscimed.2022.114777.

Kwesiga, B., Aliti, T., Nabukhonzo, P. et al. (2020). What has been the progress in addressing financial risk in Uganda? Analysis of catastrophe and impoverishment due to health payments. *BMC Health Services Research*, *20*(1), 1–8. https://doi.org/10.1186/s12913-020-05500-2.

Kwete, X., Tang, K., Chen, L. et al. (2022). Decolonizing global health: What should be the target of this movement and where does it lead us?. *Global Health Research and Policy*, *7*(1), 3. https://doi.org/10.1186/s41256-022-00237-3.

Laurell, A. C., & Arellano, O. L. (1996). Market commodities and poor relief: The World Bank proposal for health. *International Journal of Health Services*, *26*(1), 1–18. https://doi.org/10.2190/PBX9-N89E-4QFE-046V.

Lenzer, J. (2016). How Cuba eliminated mother-to-child transmission of HIV and syphilis. *British Medical Journal*, *352*. https://doi.org/10.1136/bmj.i1619.

Levine, R., & Kinder, M. (2004). *Millions saved: Proven successes in global health*. Washington, DC: Centre for Global Development.

Litsios, S. (2002). The long and difficult road to Alma-Ata: A personal reflection. *International Journal of Health Services*, *32*(4), 709–32. https://doi.org/10.2190/RP8C-L5UB-4RAF-NRH2.

Lohman, N., Hagopian, A., Luboga, S. A. et al. (2017). District health officer perceptions of PEPFAR's influence on the health system in Uganda, 2005-2011. *International Journal of Health Policy and Management*, *6*(2), 83. https://doi.org/10.15171/ijhpm.2016.98.

Lozano, R., Fullman, N., Mumford, J. E. et al. (2020). Measuring universal health coverage based on an index of effective coverage of health services in 204 countries and territories, 1990–2019: A systematic analysis for the Global Burden of Disease Study 2019. *The Lancet*, *396*(10258), 1250–84. https://doi.org/10.1016/S0140-6736(20)30750-9.

Luboga, S. A., Stover, B., Lim, T. W. et al. (2016). Did PEPFAR investments result in health system strengthening? A retrospective longitudinal study measuring non-HIV health service utilization at the district level. *Health Policy and Planning*, *31*(7), 897–909. https://doi.org/10.1093/heapol/czw009.

Lubogo, P., Lukyamuzi, J. E., Kyambadde, D. et al. (2021). Cost-effectiveness analysis of integrated community case management delivery models utilizing drug sellers and community health workers for treatment of under-five febrile cases of malaria, pneumonia, diarrhoea in rural Uganda. *Malaria Journal, 20*(1), 1–15. https://doi.org/10.1186/s12936-021-03944-3.

Machira, K., & Palamuleni, M. (2017). Perceived barriers associated with maternal health care service delivery in Malawi: Health personnel perspectives. *Studies on Ethno-Medicine, 11*(1), 49–54. https://doi.org/10.1080/09735070.2017.1311708.

Machira, K., & Palamuleni, M. (2018). Women's perspectives on quality of maternal health care services in Malawi. *International Journal of Women's Health, 10*, 25. https://doi.org/10.2147/IJWH.S144426.

Mackintosh, M., & Koivusalo, M. (2005). *Commercialization of health care.* London: Palgrave Macmillan.

Marathe, S., Hunter, B. M., Chakravarthi, I., Shukla, A., & Murray, S. F. (2020). The impacts of corporatisation of healthcare on medical practice and professionals in Maharashtra, India. *BMJ Global Health, 5*(2). https://doi.org/10.1136/bmjgh-2019-002026.

Martens, J., & Seitz, K. (2015). *Philanthropic power and development: Who shapes the agenda.* https://archive.globalpolicy.org/images/pdfs/GPFEurope/Philanthropic_Power_online.pdf.

Masefield, S. C., Msosa, A., & Grugel, J. (2020). Challenges to effective governance in a low income healthcare system: A qualitative study of stakeholder perceptions in Malawi. *BMC Health Services Research, 20*(1), 1–16. https://doi.org/10.1186/s12913-020-06002-x.

Maurrasse, D. J. (2021). *Strategic community partnerships, philanthropy, and nongovernmental organization.* Cheltenham: Edward Elgar.

Mayora, C., Kitutu, F. E., Kandala, N. B. et al. (2018). Private retail drug shops: What they are, how they operate, and implications for health care delivery in rural Uganda. *BMC Health Services Research, 18*(1), 1–12. https://doi.org/10.1186/s12913-018-3343-z.

Mbonye, A. K., Buregyeya, E., Rutebemberwa, E. et al. (2016). Prescription for antibiotics at drug shops and strategies to improve quality of care and patient safety: A cross-sectional survey in the private sector in Uganda. *BMJ open, 6*(3), e010632. https://doi.org/10.1136/bmjopen-2015-010632.

McPake, B., Hanson, K., & Mills, A. (1993). Community financing of health care in Africa: An evaluation of the Bamako initiative. *Social Science & Medicine, 36*(11), 1383–95. https://doi.org/10.1016/0277-9536(93)90381-D.

Mgawadere, F., Unkels, R., Kazembe, A., & van den Broek, N. (2017). Factors associated with maternal mortality in Malawi: Application of the three delays model. *BMC Pregnancy and Childbirth*, *17*(1), 1–9. https://doi.org/10.1186/s12884-017-1406-5.

Ministry of Health Rwanda (2018). *Fourth health sector strategic plan*. www.childrenandaids.org/sites/default/files/2018-05/Rwanda_Nat%20Health%20Sector%20Plan_2018-2024.pdf.

Ministry of Health Sri Lanka (2012). *National policy on maternal and child health*. Colombo: Government of Sri Lanka. www.health.gov.lk/moh_final/english/public/elfinder/files/publications/publishpolicy/4_Maternal%20and%20Child%20Health.pdf.

Ministry of Health Sri Lanka (2018). *National health accounts Sri Lanka 2014, 2015, 2016*. Ministry of Health, Colombo. www.health.gov.lk/moh_final/english/public/elfinder/files/publications/2019/National%20Health%20Accounts%202014-15-16%20-D8-%20Justified.pdf.

Ministry of Health Sri Lanka (2019). *Annual health statistics 2017*. Ministry of Health, Nutrition and Indigenous Medicine, Colombo. www.health.gov.lk/moh_final/english/public/elfinder/files/publications/AHB/2017/AHS2017.pdf.

Moulaert, F., MacCallum, D., & Hillier, J. (2013). Social innovation: Intuition, precept, concept. In F. Moulaert, D. MacCallum, A. Mehmood, & A. Hamdouch, eds., *The international handbook on social innovation: Collective action, social learning and transdisciplinary research*. Cheltenham: Edward Elgar, pp. 13–24.

Muangman, D. (1987). Prince Mahidol – Father of public health and modern medicine in Thailand. *Asia Pacific Journal of Public Health*, *1*(4), 72–5. https://doi.org/10.1177/101053958700100416.

Muldoon, L. K., Hogg, W. E., & Levitt, M. (2006). Primary care (PC) and primary health care (PHC): What is the difference? *Canadian Journal of Public Health*, *97*, 409–411. https://doi.org/10.1007/BF03405354.

National Institute of Statistics of Rwanda, Ministry of Health Rwanda, and ICF (2020). *Rwanda demographic and health survey 2019–20*. Kigali: National Institute of Statistics of Rwanda and ICF. https://dhsprogram.com/pubs/pdf/FR370/FR370.pdf.

Navarro, V. (1972). Health, health services, and health planning in Cuba. *International Journal of Health Services*, *2*(3), 397–432. https://doi.org/10.2190/TEKD-VG08-7M7D-5X3H.

Nithiapinyasakul, A., Arora, R., & Chamnan, P. (2016). Impact of a 20-year collaborative approach to increasing the production of rural doctors in Thailand. *International Journal of Medical Education*, *7*, 414–16. https://doi.org/10.5116/ijme.582f.4d3b.

Noree, T., Hanefeld, J., & Smith, R. (2016). Medical tourism in Thailand: A cross-sectional study. *Bulletin of the World Health Organization*, *94*(1), 30–6. https://doi.org/10.2471/BLT.14.152165.

Odhiambo, J., Rwabukwisi, F. C., Rusangwa, C. et al. (2017). Health worker attrition at a rural district hospital in Rwanda: A need for improved placement and retention strategies. *Pan African Medical Journal*, *27*(1). https://doi.org/10.11604/pamj.2017.27.168.11943.

Ojeda, M. R., Bermejo, P. M., Serrate, F. C. P. et al. (2018). Transformations in the health system in Cuba and current strategies for its consolidation and sustainability. *Rev Panam Salud Publica*, *42*, e25. https://doi.org/10.26633/RPSP.2018.25.

One Family Health (n.d.). http://onefamilyhealth.org/.

Oxfam (2012). *Salt, sugar, and malaria pills: How the Affordable Medicine Facility–Malaria endangers public health*. Oxford: Oxfam GB. https://oxfamilibrary.openrepository.com/bitstream/handle/10546/249615/bp163-affordable-medicine-facility-malaria-241012-summ-en.pdf?sequence=8.

Pagaiya, N., Kongkam, L., & Sriratana, S. (2015). Rural retention of doctors graduating from the rural medical education project to increase rural doctors in Thailand: A cohort study. *Human Resources for Health*, *13*(1), 1–8. https://doi.org/10.1186/s12960-015-0001-y.

Pagaiya, N., & Noree, T. (2009). *Thailand's health workforce: A review of challenges and experiences*. Washington, DC: World Bank. https://documents1.worldbank.org/curated/en/453661468171879780/pdf/546330WP0THLHe10Box349423B01PUBLIC1.pdf.

Pagaiya, N., Noree, T., Hongthong, P. et al. (2021). From village health volunteers to paid care givers: The optimal mix for a multidisciplinary home health care workforce in rural Thailand. *Human Resources for Health*, *19*(1), 1–10. https://doi.org/10.1186/s12960-020-00542-3.

Pagaiya, N., Sriratana, S., Wongwinyou, K., Lapkom, C., & Worarat, W. (2012). Impacts of financial measures on rural retention of doctors. *Journal of Health Systems Research*, *6*(2), 228–35.

Pangu, K. A. (1997). The Bamako initiative. *World Health*, *50*(5), 26–7. https://apps.who.int/iris/bitstream/handle/10665/330655/WH-1997-Sep-Oct-p26-27-eng.pdf.

Patcharanarumol, W., Tangcharoensathien, V., Limwattananon, S. et al. (2011). Why and how did Thailand achieve good health at low cost? In D. Balabanova, M. McKee & A. Mills, eds., *'Good health at low cost' 25 years on: What makes a successful health system?* London: The London School of Hygiene & Tropical Medicine, pp. 193–233. https://ghlc.lshtm.ac.uk/files/2011/10/GHLC-book.pdf.

Pathmanathan, I, Liljestrand, J., Martins, J. M. et al. (2003). *Investing in maternal health in Malaysia and Sri Lanka*. Washington, DC: World Bank. https://open knowledge.worldbank.org/bitstream/handle/10986/14754/259010REP LACEM10082135362401PUBLIC1.pdf?sequence=1&isAllowed=y.

Patnaik, P. (1973). On the political economy of underdevelopment. *Economic and Political Weekly*, *8*(4/6), 197–212.

Perera, P. D. A. (1985). Health care systems of Sri Lanka. In S. B. Halstead, J. A. Walsh & K. S. Warren, eds., *Good health at low cost*. New York: The Rockefeller Foundation, pp. 93–110

Perera, C., Bakrania, S., Ipince, A. et al. (2022). Impact of social protection on gender equality in low-and middle-income countries: A systematic review of reviews. *Campbell Systematic Reviews*, *18*(2), e1240. https://doi.org/10.1002/cl2.1240.

Pfotenhauer, S. M., & Juhl, J. (2017). Innovation and the political state: Beyond the myth of technologies and markets. In B. Godin & D. Vinck, eds., *Critical studies of innovation*. Cheltenham: Edward Elgar, pp. 68–93.

Phillis, J. A., Deiglmeier, K., & Miller, D. T. (2008). Rediscovering social innovation. *Stanford Social Innovation Review*, *6*(4), 34–43. https://doi.org/10.48558/GBJY-GJ47.

Pilkington, V., Keestra, S. M., & Hill, A. (2022). Global COVID-19 vaccine inequity: Failures in the first year of distribution and potential solutions for the future. *Frontiers in Public Health*, *10*. https://doi.org/10.3389%2Ffpubh.2022.821117.

Pineo, R. (2019). Cuban public healthcare: A model of success for developing nations. *Journal of Developing Societies*, *35*(1), 16–61. https://doi.org/10.1177/0169796X19826731.

Pongpirul, K. (2020). Village health volunteers in Thailand. In H. B. Perry, ed., *Health for the people: National community health worker programs from Afghanistan to Zimbabwe*, pp. 395–404. www.humanitarianlibrary.org/sites/default/files/2021/07/PA00WKKN.pdf.

Prakongsai, P. (2005). Private practice among public medical doctors. In S. Nitayarumphong, A. Mills, Y. Pongsupap & V. Tangcharoensathien, eds., *What is talked about less in health care reform?* Thailand: National Health Security Office, pp. 95–109.

Prashad, V. (2014). *The poorer nations: A possible history of the global south*. London: Verso.

Regional Committee for Africa, 49 (1999). *Review of the implementation of the Bamako Initiative*. WHO Regional Office for Africa. https://apps.who.int/iris/handle/10665/1937.

Ridde, V., Antwi, A. A., Boidin, B. et al. (2018). Time to abandon amateurism and volunteerism: Addressing tensions between the Alma-Ata principle of community participation and the effectiveness of community-based health insurance in Africa. *BMJ Global Health*, *3*(Suppl 3), e001056. https://doi.org/10.1136/bmjgh-2018-001056.

Rodriguez, F. V., Lopez, N. B., & Choonara, I. (2008). Child health in Cuba. *Archives of Disease in Childhood*, *93*(11), 991–3. http://dx.doi.org/10.1136/adc.2007.131615.

Rosenfield, A., & Min, C. J. (2009). Maternal and child health: global challenges, programs, and policies. In John Ehiri, ed., *A history of international cooperation in maternal and child health*. Boston, MA: Springer, pp. 3–17.

Rowden, R. (2013). The ghosts of user fees past: Exploring accountability for victims of a 30-year economic policy mistake. *Health & Human Rights*, *15*(1), 175.

Ruckert, A., & Labonté, R. (2014). Public–private partnerships (PPPs) in global health: The good, the bad and the ugly. *Third World Quarterly*, *35*(9), 1598–614. https://doi.org/10.1080/01436597.2014.970870.

Said Business School (2023). *Skoll Centre for Social Entrepreneurship*. www.sbs.ox.ac.uk/research/centres-and-initiatives/skoll-centre-social-entrepreneurship.

Salmon, J. W., & Thompson, S. L. (2020). *The corporatization of American health care: The rise of corporate hegemony and the loss of professional autonomy*. Cham, Switzerland: Springer Nature.

Sanders, D., Nandi, S., Labonté, R., Vance, C., & Van Damme, W. (2019). From primary health care to universal health coverage – one step forward and two steps back. *The Lancet*, *394*(10199), 619–21. https://doi.org/10.1016/S0140-6736(19)31831-8.

Segal, S. J. (1980). Preface to Health and population in developing countries: Selected papers originally presented at the Bellagio Conference, April 18-21, 1979 held under the auspices of the Rockefeller Foundation. *Social Science & Medicine*, *14c*, 61.

Sell, S. K. (2019). 21st-century capitalism: Structural challenges for universal health care. *Globalization and Health*, *15*(1), 1–9. https://doi.org/10.1186/s12992-019-0517-3.

Senanayake, H., Goonewardene, M., Ranatunga, A. et al. (2011). Achieving millennium development goals 4 and 5 in Sri Lanka. *BJOG: An International Journal of Obstetrics & Gynaecology*, *118*, 78–87. https://doi.org/10.1111/j.1471-0528.2011.03115.x.

Serrate, P. C. F. (2019). Universal health in Cuba: Healthy public policy in all sectors. *MEDICC Review*, *21*, 74–7. https://doi.org/10.37757/MR2019.V21.N4.13.

Silva, K. T. (2014). *Decolonization, development and disease: A social history of malaria in Sri Lanka*. New Delhi: Orient Blackswan.

Smith, O. (2018). *Sri Lanka: Achieving pro-poor universal health coverage without health financing reforms*. Washington, DC: World Bank Group. https://docu ments1.worldbank.org/curated/en/138941516179080537/pdf/Sri-Lanka-Achieving-pro-poor-universal-health-coverage-without-health-financing-reforms.pdf.

Smithers, D., & Waitzkin, H. (2022). Universal health coverage as hegemonic health policy in low-and middle-income countries: A mixed-methods analysis. *Social Science & Medicine*, *302*, 114961. https://doi.org/10.1016/j .socscimed.2022.114961.

Stanford Graduate School of Business (n.d.). *Centre for social innovation*. www.gsb.stanford.edu/faculty-research/centers-initiatives/csi.

Stein, F., & Sridhar, D. (2018). The financialisation of global health. *Wellcome Open Research*, *3*, 17. https://doi.org/10.12688/wellcomeopenres.13885.1.

Sundararaman, T. (2018). How Thailand built a universal healthcare system without giving private sector free rein. *Scroll.in* 20 February. https://scroll.in/ pulse/869171/thailand-built-a-universal-healthcare-system-without-giving-private-sector-free-rein.

Swanson, K. A., Swanson, J. M., Gill, A. E., & Walter, C. (1995). Primary care in Cuba: A public health approach. *Health Care for Women International*, *16*(4), 299–308. https://doi.org/10.1080/07399339509516183.

Tangcharoensathien, V., Witthayapipopsakul, W., Panichkriangkrai, W., Patcharanarumol, W., & Mills, A. (2018). Health systems development in Thailand: A solid platform for successful implementation of universal health coverage. *The Lancet*, *391*(10126), 1205–23. https://doi.org/10.1016/S0140-6736(18)30198-3.

Taylor, L. (2022). Covid-19: Cuba will request WHO approval for homegrown vaccine. *British Medical Journal*, *376*, o23. https://doi.org/10.1136/bmj .o230.

TDR (2017). *Private drug shops providing care for young children*. https://tdr .who.int/newsroom/news/item/29-03-2017-private-drug-shops-providing-care-for-young-children.

TDR (2021). *Social innovation in health initiative*. https://socialinnovationin health.org/.

ThinkWell (2020). *How primary health care services are financed in Uganda: A review of the purchasing landscape*. https://thinkwell.global/wp-content/ uploads/2020/09/Uganda-Policy-Review_Final_18-Sept-2020-Final-.pdf.

Tougher, S., Ye, Y., Amuasi, J. H. et al. (2012). Effect of the Affordable Medicines Facility – Malaria (AMFm) on the availability, price, and market

WHO (2020c). *Children: Improving survival and well-being.* www.who.int/
news-room/fact-sheets/detail/children-reducing-mortality.

WHO (2023). *Reorienting health systems to primary health care as a resilient
foundation for universal health coverage and preparations for a high-level
meeting of the United Nations General Assembly on universal health coverage.* https://apps.who.int/gb/ebwha/pdf_files/EB152/B152_5-en.pdf.

WHO (n.d.). *Maternal mortality in 2000-2017 Malawi.* https://cdn.who.int/
media/docs/default-source/gho-documents/maternal-health-countries/mater
nal_health_mwi_en.pdf.

WHO CMH (2001). *Macroeconomics and health: Investing in health for
economic development. Report of the Commission on Macroeconomics and
Health.* https://apps.who.int/iris/bitstream/handle/10665/42435/9241545
50X.pdf?sequence=1&isAllowed=y.

WHO CSDOH (2008). *Closing the gap in a generation: Health equity through
action on the social determinants of health.* https://apps.who.int/iris/rest/
bitstreams/65985/retrieve.

WHO-UNICEF (1978). *Primary health care: A joint report / by the Director-
General of the world health organization and the executive director of the
united nations children's fund.* https://apps.who.int/iris/handle/10665/39225.

WHO/UNICEF (2012). *WHO/UNICEF joint statement: Integrated community
case management.* www.childhealthtaskforce.org/sites/default/files/2019-
07/iCCM%28WHO%2C%20UNICEF%2C%202012%29.pdf.

WHO & UNICEF (2018). *Declaration of Astana.* www.who.int/publications/i/
item/WHO-HIS-SDS-2018.61.

WHO/UNICEF (2020). *Institutionalizing integrated community case management (iCCM) to end preventable child deaths.* www.who.int/publications/i/
item/9789240006935.

WHO & World Bank (2014). *Monitoring progress towards universal health
coverage at country and global levels: Framework, measures and targets.*
http://apps.who.int/iris/bitstream/handle/10665/112824/WHO_HIS_HIA_
14.1_eng.pdf?sequence=1.

WHO & World Bank (2017). *Healthy systems for universal health coverage:
A joint vision for healthy lives.* www.uhc2030.org/fileadmin/uploads/
uhc2030/Documents/About_UHC2030/mgt_arrangemts___docs/
UHC2030_Official_documents/UHC2030_vision_paper_WEB2.pdf.

WHO & World Bank (2021). *Tracking universal health coverage: 2021 global
monitoring report.* www.who.int/publications/i/item/9789240040618.

Wibulpolprasert, S., & Pengpaibon, P. (2003). Integrated strategies to tackle the
inequitable distribution of doctors in Thailand: Four decades of experience.

Human Resources for Health, 1(1), 1–17. https://doi.org/10.1186/1478-4491-1-12.

Wibulpolprasert, S., & Fleck, F. (2014). Thailand's health ambitions pay off. *Bulletin of the World Health Organization, 92*(7), 472–3. doi: 10.2471/BLT.14.030714.

Wickramasinghe, N. (2006). *Sri Lanka in the modern age: A history of contested identities.* Honolulu: University of Hawaii Press.

Wiist, W. (2011). *Philanthropic foundations and the public health agenda.* New York: Corporations and Health Watch.

World Bank (1987). *Financing health services in developing countries.* Washington, DC: World Bank. https://documents1.worldbank.org/curated/en/468091468137379607/pdf/multi-page.pdf.

World Bank (1993). *World development report 1993: Investing in health.* New York: Oxford University Press. https://openknowledge.worldbank.org/bitstream/handle/10986/5976/WDR%201993%20-%20English.pdf?sequence=1&isAllowed=y.

World Bank (2016). *UHC in Africa: A framework for action.* https://documents1.worldbank.org/curated/en/735071472096342073/pdf/108008-v1-REVISED-PUBLIC-Main-report-TICAD-UHC-Framework-FINAL.pdf.

World Bank (2021). *Walking the talk: Reimagining primary health care after COVID-19.* https://openknowledge.worldbank.org/bitstream/handle/10986/35842/9781464817687.pdf?sequence=7&isAllowed=y.

World Bank (2023). *World Bank open data.* https://data.worldbank.org/.

World Bank (n.d.a). *World Bank country and lending groups.* https://datahelpdesk.worldbank.org/knowledgebase/articles/906519.

World Bank (n.d.b). *The World Bank in Thailand.* www.worldbank.org/en/country/thailand/overview.

Xue, Y., Smith, J. A., & Spetz, J. (2019). Primary care nurse practitioners and physicians in low-income and rural areas, 2010-2016. *JAMA, 321*(1), 102–5. https://doi.org/10.1001/jama.2018.17944.

Acknowledgements

We thank the following individuals for generously sharing their time and expertise in reviewing sections of the manuscript: Benjamin Chemouni, Somsak Chunharas, Laura Nervi, Sarah Rudrum, T. Sundararaman, and Jannah Wigle. We are grateful to the anonymous reviewers for their insightful comments, suggestions, and words of encouragement.

Cambridge Elements ≡

Global Development Studies

Peter Ho
Zhejiang University

Peter Ho is Distinguished Professor at Zhejiang University and high-level National Expert of China. He has held or holds the position of, amongst others, Research Professor at the London School of Economics and Political Science and the School of Oriental and African Studies, Full Professor at Leiden University and Director of the Modern East Asia Research Centre, Full Professor at Groningen University and Director of the Centre for Development Studies. Ho is well-cited and published in leading journals of development, planning and area studies. He published numerous books, including with *Cambridge University Press, Oxford University Press*, and *Wiley-Blackwell*. Ho achieved the William Kapp Prize, China Rural Development Award, and European Research Council Consolidator Grant. He chairs the International Conference on Agriculture and Rural Development (www.icardc.org) and sits on the boards of Land Use Policy, Conservation and Society, China Rural Economics, Journal of Peasant Studies, and other journals.

Servaas Storm
Delft University of Technology

Servaas Storm is a Dutch economist who has published widely on issues of macroeconomics, development, income distribution & economic growth, finance, and climate change. He is a Senior Lecturer at Delft University of Technology. He obtained a PhD in Economics (in 1992) from Erasmus University Rotterdam and worked as consultant for the ILO and UNCTAD. His latest book, co-authored with C.W.M. Naastepad, is *Macroeconomics Beyond the NAIRU* (Harvard University Press, 2012) and was awarded with the 2013 Myrdal Prize of the European Association for Evolutionary Political Economy. Servaas Storm is one of the editors of *Development and Change* (2006-now) and a member of the Institute for New Economic Thinking's Working Group on the Political Economy of Distribution.

Advisory Board

Arun Agrawal, *University of Michigan*
Jun Borras, *International Institute of Social Studies*
Daniel Bromley, *University of Wisconsin-Madison*
Jane Carruthers, *University of South Africa*
You-tien Hsing, *University of California, Berkeley*
Tamara Jacka, *Australian National University*

About the Series

The Cambridge Elements on Global Development Studies publishes ground-breaking, novel works that move beyond existing theories and methodologies of development in order to consider social change in real times and real spaces.

Cambridge Elements $\equiv$

Global Development Studies

Elements in the Series

Temporary Migrants from Southeast Asia in Australia: Lost Opportunities
Juliet Pietsch

Mobile (for) Development: When Digital Giants Take Care of Poor Women
Marine Al Dahdah

Displacement in War-torn Ukraine: State, Dislocation and Belonging
Viktoriya Sereda

Investor States: Global Health at the End of Aid
Benjamin M. Hunter

Global Health Worker Migration: Problems and Solutions
Margaret Walton-Roberts

Going Public: The Unmaking and Remaking of Universal Healthcare
Ramya Kumar and Anne-Emanuelle Birn

Milton Keynes UK
Ingram Content Group UK Ltd.
UKHW020750080124
435661UK00018B/1347

9 781009 209571